Bed & Champagne

Top Romantic Hideaways

OTHER WORKS BY BRADLEY S. O'LEARY

POLITICAL

Presidential Follies (with Ralph Z. Hallow)
Are You a Conservative or a Liberal? (with Victor Kamber)
Top 200 Reasons <u>Not</u> to Vote for Bill Clinton

TRAVEL

*Dining By Candlelight: America's 200 Most Romantic
    Restaurants*

VIDEO BOOKS

The Planet is Alive (the story of Pope John Paul)
        (Co-produced with Robert Evans)
Ronald Reagan: Story of an American President

Bed & Champagne

Top Romantic Hideaways

Bradley S. O'Leary

BORU BOOKS

Bed & Champagne: Top Romantic Hideaways © 1996 by Boru
Publishing with Bradley S. O'Leary

Library of Congress Cataloging in Publication Data is available.

ISBN 1-887161-08-2

Published in the United States by
Boru Publishing, Inc.
12004-B Commonwealth Way
Austin, TX 78759

Distributed to the trade by
National Book Network, Inc.
4720 Boston Way
Lanham, MD 20706

Boru books are available in quantity for promotional or
premium use. For information on discounts and terms, please
write to Director of Special Sales, Boru Publishing, Inc.,
12004-B Commonwealth Way, Austin, TX 78759.

Cover design by Christine Swernoff
Text design by Joyce C. Weston

Manufactured in the United States of America

98 97 96   5 4 3 2 1

To Wayne LaPierre in appreciation for his
help and work in ensuring that this book reach
an editor.

To Erin O'Leary for her research work and
inspiration.

DISCLAIMER

Readers are advised that hotel rates fluctuate in the course of time, and travel information changes under the impact of the varied and volatile factors that affect industry. Although every effort has been made to ensure the correctness of the information in this book, the publisher and author do not assume, and hereby disclaim, any liability to any party for any loss or damage caused by errors, omissions, misleading information, or any potential problem caused by information in this guide, even if such errors or omissions are a result of negligence, accident, or any other cause.

Foreword *by Laura McKenzie*

For years, I have prided myself on trying to learn everything there is to know about travel in the United States and around the world. During that time, I wrote 38 award-winning travel videos, produced a travel radio show for the NBC Mutual Radio Network, hosted several travel and adventure television programs, and appeared on *Entertainment Tonight* and *Oprah* as a travel expert.

I wanted my new series of travel books to have the same style and excellence that my videos, radio, and television have been known for. There is, however, one area of travel that over the last ten years I've turned to an expert on to give me advice—romantic places to dine, romantic hotels, romantic rooms, even the most romantic tables. My husband David and I travel a lot on business, but we try to mix in as much romance as we can. The expert we've always turned to is a good friend of ours who has traveled with us on a number of occasions and who always amazes us with his ongoing quest for romantic places and romantic moments—Bradley O'Leary.

I'll give you a few examples.

We were in Cape Town, South Africa, one time, and he didn't feel the gorgeous hotel we were in was quite romantic enough for Cape Town, so he spent the day traveling the city until he found a hotel that met his romantic "standards." It's a hotel with only eight rooms, but is spectacular and very romantic! It's called the Ellerman House.

When we went to Paris and wanted a romantic restaurant, he told us to try Chez Raspoutine, a restaurant he believed to be one of the five most romantic restaurants in the world. Raspoutin is not in any guide books, and it more than lived up to Brad's build-up. We've been with Brad O'Leary when he didn't think a restaurant was romantic enough so he hired a violinist to play at our table. We've gone to a restaurant for dinner and the maitre d' would tell us Brad had been in the afternoon to move tables around so we could get a better view of the sea. We've been with him in Africa where, with a full moon at midnight, surrounded by prowling lions, leopards, and elephants, he has insisted on stopping the Land Rover so he could break out a bottle of champagne and further enjoy the evening.

His idea of the ultimate picnic for two is to show up in the middle of a forest where a caterer has laid out a spread and a string-quartet is playing. Another would be a champagne lunch set up in a hot air balloon.

We've come to believe that Brad O'Leary knows more about the magic of romance and the poetry of life than anyone we've ever met. And you certainly wouldn't expect it from looking at him. He's been a professional gambler, a political consultant, a newsletter publisher, an executive producer of movies and television shows, and he has his own nationally-syndicated radio show which airs on many NBC stations. But he's also experienced life to the fullest, and he has the stories to prove it. He was in Cuba before Castro, and worked to free the Marielitos. He has roamed the hills of Afghanistan with the Mujahideen. He was recalled to active duty with a Phantom fighter group when the Berlin Wall went up, and crossed the wall thirteen times helping refugees escape. He was in Vietnam in 1963 and 1964 helping refugees, and for a time helped run orphanages in Saigon and Macao. He was in Russia two weeks after the coup failed, helping to create a free political party system. We've met a lot of people who have told us Brad O'Leary stories, and they come from all walks of life. They might be a Vietnam war hero, like U.S. Senator John McCain

from Arizona, or former State Treasurer and U.S. Senator
from Texas, Kay Bailey Hutchison. You can hear stories
from former Vice President Dan Quayle, and you can
hear stories from three people who were in the 1996 presidential race: Pat Buchanan, U.S. Senator Phil Gramm,
and former U.S. Senator Bob Dole. You can hear the
stories from celebrities, including Robert Stack, Louise
Mandrell, Erik Estrada, Chuck Norris, and Paul Sorvino,
or one of Brad's best friends and Hollywood's most
controversial, Bob Evans, the former CEO of Paramount.

People will tell you that he's enriched their lives by
knowing him, and he's brought romance and poetry into
everything he's done with them. I hope that through this
book on romantic places to stay, you'll become as
enchanted with him as his friends and his former lovers,
and that your life will become enriched with just a little
more romance.

What is a Romantic Interlude?

WHAT IS ROMANCE?

Romance is a mood, and we create it—we make it happen. We can turn the most dismal experience into a romantic one if we work at it. Romance comes alive when you awaken the five senses.

Romance is thrilling the sense of sight by wrapping a gift in a package, by calling ahead and having flowers delivered to your room or your table at dinner. Romance is packing candles when you travel so you can enjoy the soft glow of candlelight when you turn out the lights. Or you can play with the lighting, dimming it to an intimate softness, or putting in a colored light bulb (I prefer rose-tinted).

Romance is thrilling the sense of touch by stroking someone's hand or gently touching them to let them know you're there. Or it could be silk sheets on the bed, or standing on the balcony and feeling a breeze caress you, or the touch of a hot shower or gentle massage. It could be a simple bottle of scented massage or bath oil. Or you might want to spread rose petals on the bed.

Romance is thrilling the sense of smell with fresh flowers, or biscuits freshly baked in the morning. The smell of the ocean, or the scent of incense you remembered to bring along for just the right aroma. But be careful with incense. One time in a London hotel room I set off the silent smoke alarm. Perhaps I had lit too many sticks, and I had ignored the ringing telephone. Imagine my surprise when three firemen started beating on my door!

Romance is thrilling the sense of taste with each other's lips. Perhaps it's the wonderful meal you've just enjoyed, or perhaps you remembered to pack the chocolates or sweets your lover particularly likes and put on her pillow at night. You may have called ahead to make sure that her favorite white wine was chilled so it has just the right taste when it rolled over her lips. Perhaps you ordered strawberries from room service, and when you shared a kiss you placed the strawberries between your lips and savored the taste and the juices.

Romance is thrilling the sense of hearing. The sounds of the night, the crash of ocean waves, or gentle mountain breezes. Finding a perfect radio station the two of you can share. Or try buying a CD alarm clock and bring your favorite romantic CDs along with you. My favorite is Barry White's *Love is the Unicorn*. Your lover can thrill to the sound of your voice telling her how beautiful she is, or expressing your most intimate thoughts. If you are too shy, try memorizing some of the poetry in this book and tell her the words she desires to hear.

Romance can happen anywhere, if you awaken the five senses of love.

A romantic interlude is a trip to someplace extraordinary, special, warm, and inviting. It is an escape from the mundane and into a paradise regained. A romantic spot should have something unique to offer. Whether it's the classy Back Bay location of the Ritz in Boston or the wild natural scenery of The Post Ranch Inn at Big Sur, a romantic destination must offer you something you don't find in your everyday life.

What makes a place romantic? Sometimes it's nature—luxurious resort comforts in a beautiful beach or mountain setting. Or it could be the glamor and excitement of city life with all the civilized pleasures a grand hotel has to offer. If you live in the city, you probably want to escape to the wild. And if you live in the country, you might be drawn to the city lights.

Romance is a mood, and like most moods it is fragile, even fickle. While it may not take much to get you into the mood, something as simple as a messy room or a surly waiter can ruin the moment. The little things are important. Attention to detail is what sets apart a pretty good hotel from an excellent one. Does the hotel offer concierge service? Is your bed turned down at night? Will room service let you order from the restaurant menus? Is your morning coffee hot or just tepid? These details add up to make the entire experience and will either enhance or detract from your visit.

Service is very important. And great service is both attentive and unobtrusive, respectful without being obsequious, warm without trying to be your next best friend. Excellent service is almost unnoticeable. You finish a course, and the plate is whisked away, your bed is made when you come back from breakfast. The concierge knows what you want, because he/she takes the time to ask. In some of the smaller inns and resorts, the owners take an active role in the day-to-day operations. This is one of the charms of staying in a smaller establishment, and while you might sacrifice some of the amenities of larger hotels, you get the feeling that you are staying in someone's own home. This kind of service cannot be taught in hotel school, nor can it be dictated by the guidelines of a corporate hierarchy. Unfortunately, for these very reasons, excellent personal service is often rare.

Luxury hotels are popping up in every city in the country. Many of them are operated by large hotel chains. There is nothing wrong with corporate hotel ownership; in fact, some fading old dowagers have been vastly improved once they have been taken over by a chain. However, you can't always judge how good a hotel is, and you certainly can't tell how romantic it is, just by the ownership. Service and amenities at chain hotels can vary widely from location to location, even within the same city. To take just a single example, one hotel company owns two properties in the same city. One of the hotels is among the finest in the country, a perfect place for a romantic city weekend. The other is about as romantic as a YMCA. Nor should you try to go by the opposite criteria. Just because a hotel is privately owned and operated doesn't mean it's romantic or even any good.

You never can tell what staying at a hotel is like just by looking at the brochures or even reading most of the tour guides. For my various business ventures, I travel a lot. And I believe there's no reason not to mix business with pleasure. Why stay at an impersonal, nondescript hotel when you can choose a charming, romantic place instead? Over the years I have learned—slowly but surely—which are the most romantic places to stay.

That's why I wrote this book. While there are scores of travel and vacation guides already out on the market, there aren't any romantic ones. Sure, there are honeymoon planners and books on romantic destinations. But there isn't a comprehensive and detailed guide to hotels and resorts in the United States based on their romantic allure.

This book includes a wide variety of romantic interludes. There are first-class hideaways, private escapes that will both pamper you and leave you alone. There are also several big city hotels, so if you're coming into town on either business or pleasure, your stay can be as romantic. I've added a few simpler inns, for people who find luxury distracting. And specialty vacations such as yacht charters and private railroad cars, and villa rentals are also listed.

While I have tried to list the most accurate and current information in this book, prices or offerings might have changed, do please call first to make sure that you can get what you want. Nothing can be more disappointing than having a particular plan in mind—say a sunset cocktail cruise or dancing to live music—only to discover upon arrival that it is no longer offered.

Romance is poetry itself, and I have included love poems in the descriptions of these romantic hideaways. Sometimes the connection between the poem and the place is obvious, other times, the poem's meaning is more cryptic or personal. But then poetry, like love, should never have to explain itself, should it? I have found that people who frequent romantic hideaways tend to like love poetry, and hope you will enjoy the selections I have included. Should you be so inclined, feel free to send me some romantic verse, either classics of great authors or your own creations, for inclusion in next year's edition.

This is the first edition of *Bed & Champagne: Top Romantic Hideaways*. Subsequent editions will include changes to the lodgings themselves, new American and international entries, and comments based on reader response. Please take this book with you on your travels. And when you find a place that is either unique and undiscovered, or terribly overrated, let me know. Use the card attached inside the back cover to note your response or send us a note on the world wide web. I'd also like to hear your answer to the age-old question—what is romance?

In the meantime, enjoy your romantic travels.

Alabama

MARRIOTT'S GRAND HOTEL
Point Clear

> There are certain ladies in our land
> Who bring to Life the gift of gay
> Uncompromising sanity.
> The past, for them, is safe and sure.
> Perhaps their only vanity
> Is that they know they can endure
> The rigours of another day.
>
> — "To L. R-M" by Noel Coward

Noel Coward wrote this verse to an English lady, but it applies just as well to a Grande Dame of the American South. The Grand Hotel is one of the South's great ladies, proving Scarlett O'Hara's hopeful promise that tomorrow is another day.

The Grand Hotel is situated on the Gulf Coast, an area rich with history, scenic beauty, and steamy romance. First opened in 1847 as the Point Clear Hotel, the original hotel was accessible only by boat. Known as "The Queen of Southern Resorts," the hotel was a favorite among the southern gentility, who enjoyed parties, balls, and high-stakes poker games there. During the Civil War, the hotel served as an encampment and field hospital for Confederate soldiers. When the hotel opened for business after the war, a fire destroyed the kitchen and the main building. No guests were harmed, but all the records from the war were lost. Now the hotel maintains a Confederate Memorial Cemetery, where 150 unknown soldiers rest.

The property changed hands several times, with new owners making several improvements, until the hotel was severely damaged by a hurricane. Soon thereafter, the hotel was bought by Marriott, which restored and improved the resort while retaining its history and charm. Now the hotel sits on 550 acres of manicured grounds, shaded by flowering magnolias and mossy oaks. Nearby are the lush foliage and charming homes of the Point Clear Historic District.

Three separate buildings offer guest accommodations overlooking the bay, marina, and surrounding gardens. All 308 rooms are newly renovated with careful attention to period detail. You can dance in the moonlight at Julep Point or go for a walk along the waterfront. Pavilion Wharf offers exceptional fishing and crab trapping, and the chef will glady prepare anything you catch. Point Clear Stables provide thoroughbred horses for riding along more than five miles of trails. Wind surfers, wave runners, and sailboats are all available for use on the bay. Lakewood Golf course offers some of the best golf in the area. And the hotel's elegant 111-foot yacht, Southern Comfort, is the place for watching a spectacular sunset, or enjoying cocktail and dinner cruises under the southern moonlight.

The Grand Dining Room is formal yet relaxed, serving lavish breakfast and luncheon buffets, along with the legendary Sunday champagne jazz brunch. The Bayview Room offers great local seafood cooked to your taste and an exquisite view of Mobile Bay. The Clubroom at the golf course provides a country club atmosphere for more casual lunches and dinners. Afternoon tea is served in the rustic elegance of the main lobby every day.

The Grand Hotel combines southern hospitality with modern comforts, offering a vast array of amenities and activities in an environment of unparalleled historic charm.

Rates: Rooms $99–$169; Suites $169–$199
     (based upon season)

MARRIOTT'S GRAND HOTEL
1 Grand Boulevard
Point Clear, AL 36564

Phone	(334) 928-9201
Toll free	(800) 544-9933
Fax	(334) 928-1149

▬▬▬▬

Alaska

KACHEMAK BAY WILDERNESS LODGE
Homer

> And the sunlight clasps the earth,
>> And the moonbeams kiss the sea:—
> What are all these kissings worth,
>> If thou kiss not me?

> — "Love's Philosophy" by Percy Bysshe Shelley

Some romantics, like Shelley, find love in wild nature. If the two of you would like to revel in the splendid isolation of the Alaskan wild country, then Kachemak Bay is the place.

Accessible only by floatplane or ferry, this wilderness resort is situated on the spectacular Kenai Peninsula. A perfect spot for nature lovers who also want some luxury, the lodge is about a half an hour from Homer, but offers all the comforts (and more) of home, while providing exciting activities in the wilds of Alaska. You can go hiking, canoeing, kayaking, and fishing. Get steamed in the sod-roofed sauna. Eat dungeness crab that was pulled out of the bay that morning, along with homemade bread baked daily.

Kachemak is a family affair, managed with friendly hospitality and attention to detail. Mike and Diane McBride have been running the lodge for more than twenty years. Mike's a member of the Explorer's Club, a former bush pilot, a licensed skipper, and an expert on Alaska's wilderness. Diane knows all about the natural history of the area. In addition to being perfect hosts, both of them are helpful guides, always willing to answer your questions about the nature and history of this fascinating region.

Each of the four log cabins has a wood-burning stove, homemade quilts, and a porch. There's a stone fireplace

3

in the main lodge, and a private outdoor hot tub and
sauna. And beyond that, nothing but spruce tree forests
and arctic beaches. The wildlife is varied—with seals, sea
birds, moose, bear, sea otters, whales, and bald eagles all
nearby. And the region is home to the world's largest
concentration of black bears. The McBrides offer
photography workshops and guided nature tours. Or you
can dig for clams and mussels on the beach. The fishing
is some of the best in the world, offering trout, salmon,
and halibut. The Kenai Peninsula is one of Alaska's most
photographed places: when you arrive there, you might
find that you recognize it from books or calendars.

Kachemak is listed in *America's Best 100* as "America's
best wilderness lodge."

Rates: $400 (all meals and guide included)
      (Season runs from May 1st–October 1st)

KACHEMAK BAY WILDERNESS LODGE
P.O. Box 956
Homer, Alaska 99603

Phone   (907) 235-8910
Fax   (907) 235-8911

▬▬▬

Arizona

ENCHANTMENT RESORT
Sedona

> "Oh! Love," they said, "is King of Kings,
>   And Triumph is his crown.
> Earth fades in flame before his wings,
>   And Sun and Moon bow down."
>
> — "Song" by Rupert Brooke

Enchantment is what you'll find here. Nestled in a dramatic box canyon in the Secret Mountain Wilderness area of Sedona's famous Red Rock country, Enchantment is a full-service resort in a dramatic desert setting. The hotel lobby is decorated with overstuffed chairs and comfortable sofas, and a nearby fireplace which you can sit by and relax in luxurious surroundings while you enjoy a cocktail. You can also sip a cocktail on one of the many patios surrounding the front of the lobby, each with a spectacular view of the desert vista.

All of the 162 rooms at Enchantment have private decks. But the fifty-six *casita* ("little house" in Spanish) suites also have kitchenettes, barbecues, fireplaces, and separate living areas. From the large decks of each casita, you can see Boynton Canyon, a natural sanctuary embraced by soaring monoliths and spectacular overhanging cliffs that reflect shades of red and orange at sunrise and sunset. Clear, sunny days paint ever-changing pictures of the lush forest and giant red rocks.

The casual elegance of the hotel lobby gives you a feeling of openness as you gaze upon the majestic red cliffs through expansive picture windows. Views from the dining room and cocktail lounge change as the day progresses. The clubhouse is centrally located on the grounds which contain decks and lounges in various key places, and a special star-gazing deck on the roof. Piano music accompanies dinner on Friday and Saturday nights. A jazz combo plays in the lounge following dinner every weekend. Western cookouts at sunset are an Enchantment specialty.

Enchantment offers twelve tennis courts, six swimming pools, outdoor jacuzzis, and a fitness center. Adjacent to the clubhouse is the Health and Healing Spa. Some of their services include: massage therapy, aroma therapy, facials, and body wraps. You can take a nature walk along many of the hiking trails. Or play a few holes on the two golf courses nearby. Horseback and jeep rides are also available.

Enchantment is located twenty-seven miles south of Flagstaff and about 125 miles north of Phoenix, near the charming community of Sedona, famous for its red rock scenery, art galleries, and new age boutiques. The resort was featured on *Lifestyles of the Rich and Famous,* which noted "Enchantment's name is no accident."

Rates: Rooms $175–$225; Casitas $335–$565
     (based upon season)

ENCHANTMENT RESORT
525 Boynton Canyon Road
Sedona, AZ 86336

Phone   (520) 282-2900
Toll free   (800) 826-4180
Fax   (520) 282-9249

▰▰▰

THE BOULDERS
Carefree

> I dare not gaze upon her face
> But left her memory in each place;
> Where'er I saw a wild flower lie
> I kissed and bade my love good-bye.
>
> — "I Hid My Love" by John Clare

Imagine coming home to the enticing fragrance and romantic warmth of a wood-burning fireplace...enjoying a room-service breakfast on your balcony overlooking the spectacular scenery of the High Sonoran Desert...or sun bathing by the pool and looking up at a mountain of boulders where a waterfall trickles down through the sun-drenched rock. That's what you get at The Boulders.

The Boulders is a desert hideaway, which blends so easily into its surroundings that it seems to be part of the natural landscape. The 136 guest quarters at The Boulders are adobe casitas, each one individually styled and shaped to fit into the terrain. Each has a patio, fireplace, wet bar, and refrigerator. The casitas are all clustered conveniently around the main lodge.

The Boulders is one of the best golf resorts in the country, its two eighteen-hole courses winning *Golf* magazine's Gold Medal Award. But there's more than just duffing. The Boulders also has six tennis courts, a health center offering personalized fitness programs, and two swimming pools. Or you can go for a trek on the hiking and jogging paths. Horseback riding, jeep tours, and hot air ballooning are also available.

But you can't just play all day. You've also got to eat. The Boulders has three restaurants. The Palo Verde serves regional cuisine enhanced by the spectacular beauty of the Sonoran terrain. Situated in the main lodge, The Latilla Room has its own waterfall. The formal room has a large picture window looking out onto a cascading water-fall and boulders. Sunday brunch features mesquite-grilled specialties served outdoors. The Boulders Club has a view of the golf course and the Sonoran foothills. Live entertainment is featured in the Discovery Lounge.

The Boulders was named favorite American resort by subscribers of *Hideaway Report* for six years in a row. They say that once you've stayed at The Boulders, it stays with you forever. If you like it enough, you can buy a house in the surrounding residential development.

Rates: Casitas $200–$580 (based upon season)

THE BOULDERS
P.O. Box 2090
34631 North Tom Darlington Drive
Carefree, AZ 85377

Phone   (602) 488-9009
Toll free   (800) 553-1717
Fax   (602) 488-4118

▬▬▬

THE PHOENICIAN
Scottsdale

> Come away, come, sweet love,
> The golden morning breaks,
> All the earth, all the air
> Of love and pleasure speaks,
> Teach thine arms then to embrace,
> And sweet rosy lips to kiss,
> And mix our souls in mutual bliss.
>
> — "To his Love" by an Anonymous Poet

This anonymous poet could have been describing a morning at The Phoenician. One of the top resorts in the country, The Phoenician offers high-class charm and luxury in the unique ambiance of the desert Southwest. The resort spreads out over 130 acres near breathtaking Camelback Mountain, just twenty-five minutes from the Sky Harbor International Airport and convenient to the Scottsdale/Phoenix metropolitan area.

The Phoenician has 476 rooms in the main hotel. Each room is spacious and comfortable, with rattan furniture, wool berber carpeting, and oversized bathrooms in Italian marble. For visitors who want more privacy, The Phoenician offers accommodations in 107 "casitas." Each casita has parking and a private entrance. After the sun sets and the night grows colder, warming up by the the fireplace may be tempting. All of the casitas are placed around the resort's gorgeous tropical Necklace Lagoon, positioned for superb views of Camelback Mountain and the spectacular sculpture fountain. Pieces from The Phoenician's $25 million art collection decorate the guest rooms and common areas.

Fine Italian and American cuisine is served in The Terrace Dining Room, where music from one of the resort's eight Steinway grand pianos plays in the background. Light from the Italian crystal chandeliers will shimmer down upon you both while you dance the night away on the marble dance floor. The Terrace offers outstanding views, and you can dine year-round on the climate-controlled patio.

Mary Elaine's is another restaurant at the resort. It offers a spectacular rooftop vista, where you can see the Valley of the Sun by day and city lights by night. Delicate French specialties are prepared tableside, and desserts are created personally by your captain.

The choices for sporting activities are wide and varied. You can swim in one of the seven swimming pools or slide down the 165-foot long waterslide. You can play on the eighteen-hole golf course or on one of the twelve tennis courts. Swimming, archery, volleyball, and golf lessons are also available. The Centre for Well-Being, a 22,000 square foot health and fitness spa, offers eight different kinds of massages, as well as facials, personal training, nutrition, and fitness counseling. There is also a beauty salon on the premises.

Rates: Rooms $150–$505; Casitas $450–$1,500
　　　(based upon season)

THE PHOENICIAN
6000 East Camelback Road
Scottsdale, AZ 85251

Phone　　　　(602) 941-8200
Toll free　　　(800) 888-8234
Fax　　　　　(602) 947-4311

California

*There are more listings from California than anywhere else,
and that's because there are more romantic places in this state
than any other in the United States. Only California has such
a vast array of natural beauty and cosmopolitan attractions.
From the sun-drenched glamor of Los Angeles to the foggy hills
of San Francisco, the warm days and starry nights of the
desert to the wind-swept beauty of the northern coast, the
dramatic mountains of the Sierras to the lush landscapes of
Napa Valley, California has everything a romantic could
possibly desire.*

AUBERGE DU SOLEIL
Rutherford

> When she rises in the morning
> I linger to watch her;
> She spreads the bath-cloth underneath the window
> And the sunbeams catch her
> Glistening white on the shoulders,
> While down her sides the mellow
> Golden shadow glows as
> She stoops to the sponge, and her swung breasts
> Sway like full-blown yellow
> Gloire de Dijon roses.
>
> — "Gloire de Dijon" by D.H. Lawrence

Just north of San Francisco, the gorgeous Napa Valley
wine country is a great place for weekend getaways or
leisurely tours. The green, rolling hills are dotted with
grape orchards, and the area is home to some of the
finest wineries and restaurants in the country. Napa and
neighboring Sonoma Valley are particularly appealing to
romantics who seek a rural landscape that can still

provide top-class food and drink. The climate is warmer and dryer than San Francisco's, an excellent escape from what is sometimes fog and chill.

Spend a season, or at least a weekend, in Provence at this cosmopolitan European-style resort. Located on thirty-three acres, high on the hilltop looking over wine vineyards, the Auberge's terra cotta buildings blend into the surrounding countryside.

It's only an hour and a half north of San Francisco, but you'll feel like you're in France. The grounds are dotted with oaks and olive trees; terraced gardens are meticulously maintained. There are thirteen cottages with fifty villa rooms and suites. Suites have fireplaces, skylights, sunken baths, and private terraces.

The Auberge has a gourmet restaurant with a rustic French Provincial motif, replete with timber ceilings, rough-hewn wood columns, a wood-burning fireplace, and antique farming implements. Local wines are featured in the extensive wine list. After dinner relax in the piano lounge with a cocktail.

The Auberge offers a special Balloon package for Thursday through Sunday. You get a top-of-the-line suite along with complimentary wine, sunrise balloon ride, and champagne brunch. It's great for a honeymoon or anniversary celebration, or any romantic interlude. The Auberge is a fantastic place to relax and simply enjoy the pleasures of life.

Rates: Rooms $175–$400; Suites $425–$1200

AUBERGE DU SOLEIL
180 Rutherford Hill Road
Rutherford, CA 94573

Phone	(707) 963-1211
Toll free	(800) 348-5406
Fax	(707) 963-8764

BOB'S AT THE BEACH
Lake Tahoe

> Come live with me and be my love,
> And we will all the pleasures prove,
> That valleys, groves, hills, and fields,
> Wood or sleepy mountains yields.
>
> — "The Passionate Shepherd to his Love"
>   by Christopher Marlowe

On the California side of Lake Tahoe, there is one very special place to stay, a vacation rental home that's as spectacular as the Sierras themselves.

Featured on *Lifestyles of the Rich and Famous,* this wet and wild 7,000 square foot, three-story beach house is located in an exclusive electronic-gated community of million dollar homes right on stunning Lake Tahoe. It's minutes away from skiing, casinos, and all the other attractions of this fantastic resort area. The house has four bedrooms, seven baths, five fireplaces, decks, a gourmet kitchen, wet bars, a boat dock, a jacuzzi, and indoor swiming pool. There's also a beautiful garden, outdoor spiral staircase, and gorgeous glass architecture.

A video is available for more details and to get a sense of how special this place really is.

Rates: House $750–$1,500 per day (based upon season)

BOB'S AT THE BEACH
P.O. Box 8096
South Lake Tahoe, CA 96158

Phone   (916) 541-3731
Fax   (916) 541-3904

CAL-A-VIE
Vista

> When Love flies in,
> Make—make no sign;
> Owl-soft his wings,
> Sand-blind his eyes;
> Sigh, if thou must,
> But seal him thine.
>
> — "When Love Flies In" by Walter De La Mare

If you have to go to a spa, it might as well be romantic. And Cal-a-Vie is about as romantic as a spa can get. A charming European-style resort set in a secluded valley north of San Diego, Cal-a-Vie offers all the health, beauty, and fitness facilities you might desire, without making you feel as if you're in boot camp.

A better part of your morning and early afternoon is spent participating in various fitness activities which include aerobics, body contouring exercises, yoga, and tai chi. You can hike in the surrounding mountains or follow a personalized exercise program, including low-impact aerobics, boxercise, circuit training, and water sports. The late afternoon can be spent indulging yourself in beauty and skin treatments, including facials and scalp cleansings, massages, and hydrotherapy. Manicures, pedicures, and hairstyling are also offered. If that's not enough, you can also play tennis or swim in the outdoor pool. You can spend your evening pleasantly, by listening to a lecture on nutrition or by learning a new healthy recipe in a cooking class.

Cal-a-Vie has one-bedroom Mediterranean-style villas. Guests include high-profile executives and celebrities. Famous visitors have included Carrie Fisher, Anjelica Houston, Michelle Pfeiffer, and Brooke Shields.

Cal-a-Vie's former chef, Rose Daly, now cooks for Oprah Winfrey, but the new chef, Greg Alario, creates delicious low-calorie menus, including spicy black bean soup and eggplant rollatini.

As *Los Angeles* magazine said about Cal-a-Vie, "One week here could tame the Terminator." One special week is set aside in October for couples only.

Rates: $3,950 a week, 6 day minimum (all inclusive)

CAL-A-VIE
2249 Somerset Road
Vista, CA 92084

Phone   (619) 945-2055
Fax   (619) 630-0074

▬▬▬▬

CHATEAU DU SUREAU
Oakhurst

> Good God, what a night that was,
> The bed was so soft, and how we clung,
> Burning together, lying this way and that,
> Our uncontrollable passions
> Flowing through our mouths.
> If I could only die that way,
> I'd say goodbye to the business of living.
>
> — Untitled by Petronius Arbiter

Located just outside the entrance to Yosemite National Park, Chateau du Sureau is a great place to use as a home base while exploring that spectacular (but often crowded) scenic area. Or you can make it a destination and spend a romantic weekend at the Chateau without venturing out. Either way, you're in for a treat.

The Chateau du Sureau is reminiscent of a luxurious hillside estate in Provence. Driving up to the Chateau's private hillside, you see wrought-iron gates topped with an elegant crest. The gates open onto grounds of a stately manor with a stucco facade and terra cotta tile roof. A valet will take your car, and your bags will be swiftly carried to your room. The hand-carved mahogany doors with brass lion-head knockers will open before you, and the Directrice will greet you warmly. There's no fussing with check-in or payment (a handwritten bill will be discreetly given to you as you leave). Instead the Directrice will make you feel right at home, and show you to your room. But you don't have to go up there yet. Take a walk around. The grounds are meticulously landscaped, with several fountains, a swimming pool, and walking paths. Pine and oak trees cover the surrounding landscape, and you can smell the wild elderberry and manzanita.

Once inside the Inn, you can see that interior design is in keeping with this rustic yet elegant French motif. The Music Room has high ceilings and a fresco portrait of owner Erna Kubin-Clanin and her family. Enjoy a glass of sherry and conversation in the Grand Salon. A fireplace burns in the sunny Breakfast Room, where the clay floor was taken from an eight-hundred-year-old French chateau.

On arriving in your room, a chambermaid will present you with a basket of gourmet treats and tea. A fire will already be burning in the fireplace. Sit down and relax; look around at the high ceilings, the fresh flowers, and great windows. Or step out onto the balcony and enjoy the view. Why would you ever want to leave?

Maybe to have dinner at Erna's Elderberry House, where award-winning French cuisine is served with an extensive wine list. Or to take a walk on the grounds, or to have a luncheon picnic, or perhaps to play a quiet game of croquet.

Rates: Rooms $310–$410 (including full European breakfast)

CHATEAU DU SUREAU
48688 Victoria Lane, Highway 41
Oakhurst, CA 93644

Phone   (209) 683-6860
Fax   (209) 683-0800

FAIRMONT HOTEL
San Francisco

> O never give the heart outright,
> For they, for all smooth lips can say,
> Have given their hearts up to the play.
> And who could play it well enough
> If deaf and dumb and blind with love?
> He that made this knows all the cost,
> For he gave all his heart and lost.
>
> — "Never Give All the Heart" by W.B. Yeats

One of the jewels of San Francisco, the Fairmont Hotel is a place of unequalled charm and sophistication, a stunning illustration of what natives and visitors alike mean when they say, "This is the city that knows how."

The cable cars stop right in front of the Fairmont, so it's convenient to downtown and Fisherman's Wharf. A short cab ride can take you to all the other attractions this great city has to offer. There are six hundred rooms in the Fairmont, sixty-two of them suites. All rooms have mini-bars.

The most famous room in this hotel is not the penthouse suite, but rather the beautiful lobby. One of the most splendid public rooms you'll ever see, the lobby has huge marbelized columns and high ceilings in silver-and-white. The comfortable furnishings are covered in red velvet. A grand staircase is the perfect stage for dramatic entrances (or exits). In the afternoon, tea is served. And a jazz combo often accompanies cocktail hour, one of the most civilized respites in this very sophisticated city.

The Fairmont has seven restaurants. The Bella Voce offers Italian cuisine served by a singing staff. The Crown combines lavish buffet meals with an exquisite view from the Hotel's perch atop Nob Hill. The Tonga Restaurant and Hurricane Bar serve Chinese and Polynesian specialties in a South Seas atmosphere. You can dance on the boat deck and thrill to the simulated indoor "thundershowers." Masons provides contemporary California cuisine.

If you don't want to leave the comfort of your room,

the Fairmont offers twenty-four-hour room service. Evening turndown, concierge, and babysitting services are also available.

Rates: Rooms $119–$359; Suites $500–$4,000

FAIRMONT HOTEL
950 Mason Street
San Francisco, CA 94108

Phone	(415) 772-5000
Toll free	(800) 527-4727
Fax	(415) 772-5013

HIGHLANDS INN
Carmel

> Love—thou art deep—
> I cannot cross thee—
> But, were there Two
> Instead of One—
> Rower, and Yacht—some sovereign Summer—
> Who knows—but we'd reach the Sun?
>
> — "Love Thou Art High" by Emily Dickinson

Here's a place to reach the sun. Perched on a pine-covered hillside south of Carmel, overlooking one of the world's most magnificent seaside vistas, Highlands Inn is situated in a gorgeous natural setting. It's considered a great hotel, rich in history and tradition. Since its opening in 1916, the Inn has been a gathering place for artists, a hideaway for celebrities, a romantic setting for weddings and honeymoons, and always a popular destination retreat.

All the accommodations are complete with fully equipped kitchens, wood-burning fireplaces, and outdoor decks or balconies. Sumptuous "spa suites" feature spacious dressing areas and jacuzzis, with plush terry cloth robes provided for your comfort. The Highlands Inn has 142 guest quarters, almost all of them with a view of the Pacific Ocean or the Carmel coastline.

There are two restaurants at the Highlands. Pacific's

Edge, run by Chef Brian Whitmer, has 180-degree views of the ocean. A long-time favorite among locals, the restaurant features seasonal menu changes and the freshest ingredients. Pacific's Edge serves California cuisine and the wine list features many local wines. There's live piano music in the dining room, and candle-light on the tables. An annual International Culinary Festival at Highlands attracts chefs and vintners from all over the world.

For more casual dining, try the California Market. It features a choice of indoor dining near the pot-bellied stove or outdoors overlooking either the pool or the ocean.

Poet Robinson Jeffers was a frequent guest at the Inn, and called the Monterey/Carmel area "the greatest meeting of land and water in the world." Nearby is Point Lobos, a favorite subject for photographer Ansel Adams. And the ocean often offers views of passing schools of whales and sea otters.

The Highlands Inn is conveniently situated near the town of Carmel, and is also close to Monterey and the Big Sur coast. Celebrities such as Barbra Streisand, John Travolta, and Clint Eastwood (the former mayor of Carmel) have stayed there.

Rates: Rooms $190–$290; Suites $375–$800
       (based upon season)

HIGHLANDS INN
P.O. Box 1700
Carmel, CA 93921

Phone	(408) 624-3801
Toll free	(800) 682-4811
Fax	(408) 626-1574

HOTEL BEL-AIR
Los Angeles

> Where, whenas Death shall all the world subdue,
>   Our love shall live, and later life renew.
>
> — "One Day I Wrote Her Name upon the Strand"
>   by Edmund Spenser

Simply one of the best hotels in the country, the Hotel Bel-Air is famous for offering comfort, convenience, and privacy in a luxurious setting. Hidden away on eleven acres in the foothills of Bel-Air, the hotel is a secure and peaceful sanctuary among the glitz and bustle of Tinseltown. Lush gardens, flowers, streams, and lawns give the Hotel Bel-Air the feeling of a tropical oasis. You'll never think you're in America's second largest city. But you're only minutes away from the shopping at Rodeo Drive, and close to Westwood, and the LA beaches.

The Restaurant (that's what it's called) is excellent, popular both with the hotel's guests and the locals, featuring California cuisine with fresh ingredients and imaginative presentations. For dining alfresco, there's the terrace, draped with bougainvillea. The floor is heated for year-round comfort and overlooks the hotel gardens and Swan Lake, home of the famous Bel-Air swans swimming among the gentle splash of a waterfall. But you don't have to leave your room to enjoy their fabulous cuisine. Room service provides a full menu, and the service is exquisite, yet discreet. Or you can lunch, Hollywood-style, by the heated pool.

Adjacent to The Restaurant is The Bar. It has a fireplace, wood paneling, and a baby grand piano. The Bar features nightly entertainment and is a favorite meeting place for guests and locals.

The Hotel Bel-Air provides luxurious comfort in unparalleled style. The hotel's ninety-two rooms are all designed individually with Mediterranean appointments. All are furnished with art and antiques, and many have woodburning fireplaces, balconies, and patios. Hotel Bel-Air's casual but refined residential mood is enhanced by the private entrances and walled patios. Despite the privacy, all of the rooms seem close to nature with beautiful views, skylights, or French doors.

The Hotel Bel-Air is a popular wedding and honeymoon site. Celebrities ranging from Joan Crawford to Farrah Fawcett have honeymooned here. But if you'd like to get married here, book well in advance.

Rates: Rooms $315–$435; Suites $495–$950
    Best Room: Tower Room overlooking Swan Lake

HOTEL BEL-AIR
701 Stone Canyon Road
Los Angeles, CA 90077

Phone   (310) 472-1211
Toll free   (800) 648-4097
Fax   (310) 476-5890

▬▬▬▬

INN ON MT. ADA
Avalon

> Is it a month since I and you
> In the starlight of Glen Dubh
> Stretched beneath a hazel bough
> Kissed from ear and throat to brow,
> Since your fingers, neck, and chin
> Made the bars that fenced me in,
> Till Paradise seemed but a wreck
> Near your bosom, brow, and neck
> And stars grew wilder, growing wise,
> In the splendour of your eyes!
>
>   — "Is it a Month" by John Synge

Paradise can be found on Catalina Island, a secluded island just twenty-six miles off the southern California coast. It's unspoiled by progress and will remain that way, because the land is deeded to an environmental foundation, which must maintain the natural condition of this breath-taking getaway. The entire island is some seventy-six square miles, mostly mountain wilderness. There are more than one hundred miles of hiking trails and sightseeing roads across the island.

The Inn on Mt. Ada rises above the community of

Avalon. When Santa Catalina was bought by the Wrigley family in 1919, William Wrigley built the Inn because his wife had wanted "a summer vacation home with green shutters." The chewing gum magnate improved the island by building public utilities, constructing resort amenities, and making it more accessible to the mainland. The Casino he erected contains the first movie theater built for the talkies and the world's largest circular ballroom. The island even served as spring training center for Wrigley's baseball team, the Cubs, from 1921 to 1951.

Once the Wrigleys died, the house was passed along to the University of Southern California, which used the island as a marine biology study center. Then the Inn was turned into a vacation resort. Now it has six rooms available for rental. Each one is individually decorated and has its own bath—two are suites with marble fireplaces. Breakfast, lunch, and dinner are included.

There are no automobiles allowed on the island, but the Inn provides golf carts for its guests. Other recreation includes: glass bottom boat trips, backcountry excursions, seal-watch tours, horseback riding, cycling, hiking, and motor treks. The beach is small but gorgeous, though the water is often too cold for swimming. Enjoy a walk in the gorgeous and well-maintained Wrigley Memorial Botanical Gardens. Watch the sunset over the Pacific or gaze at the horizon and try to see Hawaii.

This is a place to get away from it all, to enjoy a simple yet luxurious existence.

Rates: $250–$620 (based upon season)

INN ON MT. ADA
398 Wrigley Road
P.O. Box 2560
Avalon, CA 90704

Phone   (310) 510-2030
Fax   (310) 510-2237

MALIBU BEACH INN
Malibu

> She walks in beauty, like the night
> Of cloudless climes and starry skies;
> And all that's best of dark and bright
> Meet in her aspect and her eyes:
> Thus mellowed to that tender light
> Which heaven to gaudy day denies.
>
> — "She Walks in Beauty" by Lord Byron

Malibu is a place where everyone walks in beauty. This gorgeous, glamorous town is one of the most desirable places to live in southern California. And it's easy to see why. Bisected by the Pacific Coast Highway, the town is a combination of glamorous beachfront dwellings and more private residences high up in the Malibu hills. Offering a wide variety of restaurants, nightclubs, and other entertainment, there's no reason to venture beyond Malibu itself. Yet you're only minutes from Santa Monica, Venice Beach, and West Los Angeles.

The Malibu Beach Inn gives you the opportunity to live, if only for a little while, in this spectacular setting. All of the Inn's forty-seven rooms and three suites have balconies, private baths, fireplaces, refrigerators, VCRs, and wet bars, and most importantly, spectacular views of the beach and the ocean. Continental breakfast and afternoon refreshments are available. There is no dining at the Malibu Beach Inn but, fortunately, the surrounding area offers many great restaurants.

The Inn is convenient to the spectacular Getty Museum (admission is free, but make sure to call well in advance to reserve a parking space). The Inn is also close to Malibu Pier. Or you can stay close to home, sit on the beach, and look for celebrities—or simply walk in beauty with someone you love.

Rates: Rooms $145–$205; Suites $275–$295
   (based upon season)

MALIBU BEACH INN
22878 Pacific Coast Highway
Malibu, CA 90265

Phone   (310) 456-6444
Toll free   (800) 4-MALIBU
Fax   (310) 456-1499

POST RANCH INN
Big Sur

> Time was. Time is. Time shall be.
> Man invented time to be used.
> Love was. Love is. Love shall be.
> Yet man never invented love
> Nor is love to be used like time.
>
> — "Solo for Saturday Night Guitar"
> by Carl Sandburg

A dramatic coastline of mountains and cliffs rising up from the ocean. The secluded beauty of unspoiled beaches and deep forest wilderness. Brilliant sunshine, the spray of salt water, spectacular sunsets, and quiet, starry nights—that's Big Sur, an unforgettable place and one of the most unique places in the country.

The clock runs differently at Big Sur. You won't be hurried or harried. There will be no distractions or interruptions. You'll be able to enjoy each other in a peaceful "earthly" environment.

The place to stay at Big Sur is Post Ranch Inn, a romantic country inn nestled in a mountain meadow with a spectacular ocean view. The Post Ranch enjoys some of the most dramatic meetings of land and sea in the world.

The Inn is located right off Highway One in Big Sur. You can't see it from the road, but the ninety-eight-acre hideaway stretches out all the way to the ocean. When you arrive at the reception office, a van will take you up the winding road that leads to a secluded bluff where the thirty guest villas are located. Some of these are eccentrically designed, like the ones built on stilts, or covered in sod roofs. But they all blend harmoniously into the landscape, and inside they offer the most modern conveniences.

All the guest quarters have fireplaces, jacuzzis, wet bars, refrigerators, and private decks with spectacular views so you can absorb the surrounding beauty. The rooms have high ceilings and walls of stone and wood, with lots of windows to enjoy the view.

At the main lodge, a non-smoking dining room offers a gorgeous view from a huge picture window. There is also a terrace bar, with a sweeping view of the ocean and mountains. The first-rate cuisine is complemented by an extensive wine list.

There is a lot to do in Big Sur and the surrounding area. Hiking, swimming, and horseback riding are among the local activities. Or you can just kick back and do nothing at all.

Rates: $285–$545 (based upon season)

POST RANCH INN
P.O. Box 219
Big Sur, CA 93920

Phone	(408) 667-2200
Toll free	(800) 527-2200
Fax	(408) 667-2824

RITZ-CARLTON LAGUNA NIGUEL
Dana Point

> How should we like it were stars to burn
> With a passion for us we could not return?
> If equal affection cannot be,
> Let the more loving one be me.
>
> — "The More Loving One" by W.H. Auden

The stars burn with passion here in Laguna Niguel, and you will definitely find affection at this world-class hotel in a gorgeous natural setting.

The Ritz-Carlton Laguna Niguel is situated on top of a 150-foot bluff, with stunning views of the Pacific and Catalina Island. The lobby is breathtaking, with marble floors, silk tapestried walls, original artwork, and priceless antiques. A fireplace glows cozily, while beyond the arched windows the Pacific Ocean beckons.

The hotel's 393 rooms are all decorated like Mediterranean villas with pale woods and botanical prints on the walls. The furniture is French provincial, and the color schemes are seafoam green and blue. Fewer than half the rooms have an ocean view, so make sure you ask for one. And only four rooms have fireplaces. Although the weather is comfortable all year round, you might want to cozy up in front of the blazing logs of a wood fire. There are twenty-seven rooms at concierge level. Here guests receive impeccable service, including a concierge, private key access to their floor, and five meal presentations (continental breakfast, light lunch, cocktails and hors d'oeuvres, afternoon tea, and chocolates and cordials). The Presidential Suite offers a private service entrance, marble bar, and grand piano.

The best of the hotel's three restaurants is The Dining Room. But all of their menus reflect the simplicity and originality of California cuisine, featuring only the freshest local produce, herbs, seafood, and dairy products. There's music in the Club Grill & Bar and two separate lounges serve cocktails.

The hotel offers several different packages, including what is called the Ultimate Experience. This is the romantic escape of a lifetime. First a limousine picks you up at any southern California airport and whisks you off to the hotel. Upon arrival, you will be served by a personal concierge, and a dozen long-stemmed roses, a bottle of Dom Perignon champagne, and two personally monogrammed Ritz-Carlton bathrobes await you and your guest in the room. You'll also be treated to a crystal decanter and two glasses, a $500 shopping spree in the hotel shops, and unlimited use of the fitness center. Your personal concierge will be available to cater to your every need, including all three meals served in the privacy of your own suite.

There's lot's to do nearby. See the swallows return to San Juan Capistrano, the first sign of spring. Take a trip across the border to Mexico. Go to Disneyland...or not.

Visit the many galleries, shops, restaurants, and night-clubs of Laguna Beach, a lively artists' colony in staid Orange County.

The Ritz-Carlton Laguna Niguel has earned Mobil's Five Star and AAA's Five Diamond Awards.

Rates: Rooms $235–$485; Suites $415–$3,000

RITZ-CARLTON LAGUNA NIGUEL
33533 Ritz-Carlton Drive
Dana Point, CA 92629

Phone   (714) 240-2000
Toll free   (800) 241-3333
Fax   (714) 240-0829

SAN YSIDRO RANCH
Montecito

> Had we but world enough, and time,
> This coyness, Lady, were no crime.
> We would sit down and think which way
> To walk and pass our long love's day.
>
> — "To His Coy Mistress" by Andrew Marvell

There's world enough and time here, for a romantic escape. If Andrew Marvell had brought his mistress here, she would have found it impossible to resist. A French-style inn nestled in the Santa Ynez Mountains just outside Santa Barbara, San Ysidro is a comfortable and discreet hideaway for Hollywood celebrities, and business and political leaders who seek privacy and elegance in a gorgeous natural setting. Originally part of a Spanish land grant, the Santa Barbara Mission raised cattle on the San Ysidro Ranch. Later it was used as a citrus orchard. Now it is an all-purpose resort with all the modern amenities provided in a secluded country enclave.

The Ranch has 550 acres of woods, trails, and meadows. There's plenty of opportunities for hiking, tennis, swimming, riding, or just lounging around. The Plow and Angel dining room and sun deck serve breakfast, lunch, and Sunday brunch by sunlight; dinner by candlelight. The bar has live entertainment and dancing. The heated pool is open year round and has a comfortable lounging area.

Your name is engraved on a wooden sign hung outside the door of your guest cottage for the duration of your stay. Some of the cottages have private jacuzzis. All of them have fireplaces, bars, and porches with lovely views.

Guests meet at the Hacienda Lounge where morning coffee and newspapers are served, if you need to keep up with the world. In the afternoon there's an honor bar where you can mix your own drinks. The lounge also offers the Ranch's only television set, with a videocassette library containing over four hundred videos.

The ranch was once owned by Ronald Coleman, who had many of his friends come to visit. Laurence Olivier and Janet Leigh were married under the arbor in the garden. John F. Kennedy and Jackie spent their honeymoon here. JFK left a message at the front desk, saying, "No calls, please."

Rates: Rooms $295–$485; Suites $585–$1,100

SAN YSIDRO RANCH
900 San Ysidro Lane
Montecito, CA 93108

Phone	(805) 969-5046
Toll free	(800) 368-6788
Fax	(805) 565-1995

SHUTTERS ON THE BEACH
Santa Monica

> I can't hold you and I can't leave you,
>   and sorting the reasons to leave you or hold you,
>   I find an intangible one to love you,
>   and many tangible ones to forgo you.
>
> — "I Can't Hold You and I Can't Leave You"
>   by Juana Inés DeLa Cruz

The only first-class hotel in Los Angeles that is located right on the ocean, Shutters on the Beach is quickly becoming a favorite among LA visitors in the know. The area is one of the best spots for sunsets, making Shutters one of the most desirable romantic spots in southern California.

The hotel is divided into two separate structures. The main building is situated in front of the swimming pool and closer to the road. The beachfront cottages are nearer the water. You'll want a room in one of the beachfront cottages, especially since it costs the same as a room in the main building. Some rooms have fireplaces, most of them have jacuzzis. All of them have sliding shutters that open toward the beach. A fantastic collection of contemporary art is scattered throughout the property. But the most impressive amenity that Shutters has to offer is the Pacific Ocean, right on its doorstep. Here you can watch the sunset in the privacy of your own room or out in one of the hotel's cozy common areas.

Shutters' main restaurant, One Pico, offers the finest in California cuisine, along with spectacular California sunsets. One of West LA's hottest dining establishments, it features an innovative menu that specializes in seafood and other fresh ingredients. Pedals is closer to the beach itself and more laid-back, serving breakfast, lunch, and dinner, with many of its menu specialties cooked outdoors on the wood-burning grill. The Handle Bar is a great place to enjoy a cocktail and watch the sun go down. Twenty-four-hour room service is also available.

Shutters offers concierge service and evening turndown. Overnight laundry service is available, as is personal massage treatment. There's also a pool, jacuzzi, sauna, and other health and spa facilities. Beach equipment and bicycle rentals are available.

Rates: Rooms $290–$475; Suites $675–$975

SHUTTERS ON THE BEACH
1 Pico Boulevard
Santa Monica, CA 90405

Phone	(310) 458-0030
Toll free	(800) 334-9000
Fax	(310) 458-4589

THE HUNTINGTON HOTEL
San Francisco

> And the flame of the blue star of twilight, hung low on
>   the rim of the sky,
> Has awaked in our hearts, my beloved, a sadness that
>   may not die.
>
> — "The White Birds" by W.B. Yeats

Yeats could have been describing the view from The
Huntington, a vista of scenic beauty tinged with foggy
melancholy and redolent of memory, love lost and love
regained.

Perched at the top of prestigious Nob Hill, The
Huntington Hotel overlooks Huntington Park, Grace
Cathedral, and the Flood Mansion, as well as the entire
city of San Francisco. The hotel has some of the most
spectacular views in this city of spectacular views. Look
in one direction and you can see the city skyline, look in
another and there's the Bay. Cable cars ride right past the
hotel's front door, making many of the city's attractions,
like Union Square and Fisherman's Wharf, just a short
ride away.

Originally built in 1924, the twelve-story Huntington
was the first steel and brick high rise west of the
Mississippi. Now the hotel has 140 individually decorated rooms. All the rooms and suites have fabulous
views of the city or the Bay, and they're all furnished
with antiques and signature artwork. Every suite has a
wet bar, and some have kitchens.

There's a concierge on duty from 7 a.m. until 11 p.m.
The Big Four serves excellent continental cuisine in a
club-like atmosphere. Set in an elegant, early-California
decor, the warm colors, rich leather, and sparkling
beveled glass surround an incomparable selection of San
Francisco and Western memorabilia. The restaurant is
named after The Big Four railroad magnates—Stanford,
Hopkins, Crocker, and Huntington.

The Huntington offers a Romance package which
includes a luxury room, complimentary champagne, tea
or sherry service upon arrival, a chauffered limousine to

drive you around to see the city's attractions, concierge service, and privileges at Nob Hill's spa and fitness center.

Rates: Rooms $190–$240; Suites $290–$790

THE HUNTINGTON HOTEL
1075 California Street
San Francisco, CA 94108

Phone   (415) 474-5400
Toll free   (800) 227-4683
Fax   (415) 474-6227

▉▉▉▉▉▉

THE L'AUBERGE DEL MAR
Del Mar

> The mind has a thousand eyes,
> And the heart but one;
> Yet the light of a whole life dies
> When love is done.

> — "The Night Has a Thousand Eyes"
> by Francis William Bourdillon

Located in the scenic coastal town of Del Mar, only a few miles north of San Diego, the L'Auberge, which in French means "inn", opened in 1989, but has already achieved a sterling reputation for exquisite location, food, and service. The Inn was built on the site of the legendary Hotel Del Mar, a popular resort during the early years of Hollywood. Celebrity guests like Rudolph Valentino, Rita Hayworth, Bing Crosby, and Jimmy Durante enjoyed the sun and sea, while escaping the stress of stardom.

The Inn's lobby features a re-creation of the double-sided fireplace and hearth that graced the lobby of the original hotel. The lobby is the heart of the resort, where guests gather for daily afternoon tea, weekend dinner dancing, and light opera performances. There are 120 guest rooms and eight deluxe suites offering amenities such as oversized balconies with magnificent views, marble baths, mini-refrigerators, wet bars, cathedral ceilings, and fireplaces. A concierge service provides arrangements for golf, a visit to the famous Del Mar race track, hot air ballooning, beach picnics, and other excursions. Activities on the Inn's own grounds include tennis, a European health spa and baths, exercise room, lap pool, swimming pool, and jacuzzi.

For fine dining, The Dining Room is the essence of southern Californian casual elegance. A vibrant bistro ambiance is created in a sunlit garden setting. You can enjoy indoor or terrace dining next to gentle waterfalls and streams. Epicurean excellence and gracious service are the hallmarks of The Dining Room, which features superb presentations of fresh seafoods and pastas.

Rates: Rooms $159–319; Suites $500–$950

THE L'AUBERGE DEL MAR
1540 Camino Del Mar
Del Mar, California 92014

Phone	(619) 259-1515
Toll free	(800) 553-1336
Fax	(619) 755-4940

THE SHERMAN HOUSE
San Francisco

> With the earth and the sky and the water, remade, like
>   a casket of gold
> For my dreams of your image that blossoms a rose in
>   the deeps of my heart.
>
> — "The Lover Tells of the Rose in His Heart"
>   by W.B. Yeats

A restored Victorian in the elegant Pacific Heights neighborhood of San Francisco, The Sherman House offers romantic rooms with canopied four-poster beds, down comforters, and marble fireplaces. Breakfast at the Solarium is a San Francisco treat, with enchanting views of the Bay and sunlight pouring through the leaded glass. Afternoon tea is served in the gallery, a sumptuous Second Empire salon. Dinners can be taken by the open fireplace in the dining room or in the privacy of your own room. And room service is available twenty-four hours a day.

The Sherman House has fourteen rooms and suites. Once the billiard room in the Sherman mansion, the Paderewski Suite is now "the most romantic hotel suite in San Francisco," according to *Bride's* magazine. The suite has dark wood wainscoting and ebony carpet, giving the room a Jacobean look. The mahogony bed is covered with brocade curtains. There's a marble fireplace and a bay window seat with plenty of cushions for you to sit and look out onto the panoramic view of the Golden Gate Bridge, Alcatraz, and the rest of the Bay. The bathroom has a jacuzzi and its own fireplace.

The Sherman House is a great place to have a wedding. For smaller ceremonies, the gazebo in the garden can accommodate thirty guests. If your guest list is a bit larger, try the Rose Garden, which can hold up to 120 comfortably. Inside, there's the gallery, where up to thirty guests can gather in front of the fireplace for cozy nuptials. Finally the terrace offers sweeping views of the Golden Gate Bridge and the Palace of Fine Arts. It can hold up to fifty.

The Sherman House can also cater your wedding. The food and beverage manager will design just the right menu and table arrangements for you. Music can be provided by a harpist, pianist, violinist, or classical trio.

Rates: $200–$395; Suites $600–$825

THE SHERMAN HOUSE
2160 Green Street
San Francisco, CA 94123

Phone	(415) 563-3600
Toll free	(800) 424-5777
Fax	(415) 563-1882

▬▬

YACHT CHARTERS
Newport Beach

They say that having friends who own boats is better than owning one yourself. And if you don't have friends who are willing to lend you their private yacht for a romantic ocean cruise, then you can always charter one. The Affinity is available for charters along the West Coast. This ninety-eight foot boat has a main saloon, with seating, entertainment center, bar, dining facility, and en-suite aft deck. The Affinity can take you to anchorages that other yachts might miss. And in her toy box you'll find waterskis, jet skis, diving and snorkeling gear, underwater cameras, skeet shooting equipment, scooters, tennis rackets, and volleyballs for when you touch land. Relax in the full-width double bed stateroom, featuring a settee, entertainment center, and whirpool tub. Of course the boat is fully crewed, so you don't have to do anything but enjoy your private ocean voyage. To charter the Affinity contact:

YACHT CHARTERS
3471 Via Lido, Box 2268
Newport Beach, CA 92663

Phone   (714) 673-5252
Fax   (714) 673-8795

Colorado

BROWN PALACE
Denver

> And it seems, wherever I look,
> Phantoms of irreclaimable happiness taunt me.
> Then I see her, petalled in new-blown hours,
> Beside me—"All you love most there
> Has blossomed again," she murmurs, "all that you
>   missed there
> Has grown to be yours."
>
>   — "The Album" by Cecil Day Lewis

Back when Denver was still a Wild West town, the Brown
Palace was one of the few bastions of civilization. Denver
has grown up since then; now it's a world-class city. And
the Brown Palace is still one of the city's most refined
places to stay.

The Brown Palace is a national historic landmark,
and once you step inside, you'll see why. The lobby is a
nine-story atrium soaring high above you. On the ground
floor, the walls are paneled in Mexican onyx. Above, the
atrium rises past elaborate designs in the cast iron railings
at each floor. Near the top, the style changes to art deco
reflected by glass brick. Dominating the whole setting is
the stained glass ceiling, which proclaims the hotel's
Victorian heritage.

There are 230 rooms in the hotel, twenty-five of
which are suites. Each room is individual in style and
appointment, furnished with traditional decor. In larger
rooms and suites, priceless works of art complement
furnishings from around the world. All guests receive
concierge service.

Afternoon tea is served every day except Sunday, and
is accompanied by live harp music. For cocktail hour, you
can enjoy fine wines and champagnes by the glass while

listening to the lounge's pianist. The Palace Arms is recognized as one of the finest and most elegant dining rooms in Denver. Its wine list has earned awards from discriminating palettes such as *The Wine Spectator.*

Ellyngtons, the main dining room, is famous for its elaborate Dom Perignon Sunday brunch. The Ship Tavern is decorated in a nautical motif and offers local specialties like Colorado prime rib and fresh trout. Henry C's is an intimate lounge named after the hotel's founder, Henry C. Brown.

Located right in the heart of downtown Denver, the Brown Palace is a great launching point for visiting the city or heading into the mountains beyond. The hotel offers Romantic Getaway packages if you just want to stay put and enjoy the historic ambiance and great service.

Rates: Rooms $185–$205; Suites $245–$725

BROWN PALACE
321 Seventeenth Street
Denver, CO 80202

Phone   (303) 297-3111
Toll free   (800) 321-2599
Fax   (303) 293-9204

TALL TIMBER AT SAN JUAN NATIONAL FOREST
Durango

> Shall I compare thee to a summer's day?
> Thou art more lovely and more temperate:
> Rough winds do shake the darling buds of May,
> And summer's lease hath all too short a date.
>
> — "Shall I Compare Thee to a Summer's Day"
>   by William Shakespeare

Tall Timber is a great Rocky Mountain escape vacation for those seeking romantic seclusion in spectacular natural surroundings. The resort is accessible only by train or helicopter, and the only contact with the outside world is a radiophone used by the staff for arranging supplies or in case of emergency. But that doesn't mean you'll be sacrificing luxury or comfort, just escaping the stress and strain of every day life.

When you arrive at the local airport, the Tall Timber helicopter pilot is there to fly you to the resort within fifteen minutes. If you come in by narrow gauge train, staff members are at the depot to meet you. The train ride from Silverton to Durango is half the fun, as this two-hour scenic ride passes through one of the most awe-inspiring canyons in the country.

Guest accommodations at Tall Timber are ten private sleeping suites. Each suite is designed for privacy, not view, but most of the resort has views of the San Juan Forest, and the resort itself is set on 180 acres, adjacent to literally millions of acres of this scenic national park. All suites have a wet bar and a sitting area with a floor-to-ceiling stone fireplace. There are no televisions, radios, or telephones in the rooms. Two suites have whirlpools. All the rooms have contemporary furnishings of wood and brass, decorated with earth tones and natural hues. Guests receive a complimentary robe to take with them when they depart. Turndown treats are provided at night.

What are you going to do without the telephone always ringing? Well, you can go for a swim in the outdoor pool. Go fishing in the nearby trout streams. Take a jog along the nature trails. Or put on your hiking boots and go for a long walk. There's tennis courts and a nine-hole golf course. A fitness center offers hot spas and Finnish sauna (traditionally followed by a plunge in the pool). In the summer you can go horseback riding. In the winter there's snowmobiling.

Fresh wildflowers decorate the lobby and common areas. At The Dining Room each table is set in its own bay window overlooking the canyon. Candlelight and fresh flowers decorate your table. Dress is informal, and the atmosphere is one of casual rustic elegance. The Dining Room serves international cuisine with fresh fruits and vegetables, some grown in Tall Timber's own garden. The Tall Timber bakery provides fresh breads, cakes, and pastries daily. There is a cocktail lounge and roving bar cart that serves drinks all over the property, at the pool and cabana area as well as the golf course. But the only room service is continental breakfast in the morning. On Friday evening during the summer, the staff puts on a spectacular fireworks show.

A summer's day at Tall Timber is beyond comparison. Warm and sunny with low humidity and cool mountain breezes, there is nothing better. Except perhaps a Rocky Mountain summer evening. But what you do once the sun sets is up to you.

Rates: Suites $1,100–$1,600 (3 night/4 day minimum)

TALL TIMBER AT SAN JUAN NATIONAL FOREST
S.S.R. Box 90
Durango, CO 81301

Phone   (970) 259-4813

THE LITTLE NELL
Aspen

> Come live with me, and be my love,
> And we will some new pleasures prove
> Of golden sands, and crystal brooks,
> With silken lines, and silver hooks.
>
> — "The Bait" by John Donne

Aspen is one of the most romantic places in the United States. A beautiful Victorian town in the Roaring Fork River Valley, Aspen was first an Indian settlement, then a mining town, then a ghost town. After World War II, when returning alpine soldiers brought the European ski craze back to the States, Aspen became one of the finest Western ski resorts. And now, despite its reputation as Hollywood in the Rockies, Aspen has still retained all of its rugged mountain charm.

The Little Nell is located at the base of Ajax mountain, one of the toughest ski slopes to get to without a helicopter. Adjacent to Silver Queen gondola, and just seventeen steps away from the slopes, this is the only "ski in/ski out" luxury hotel in town. Guests at The

Little Nell enjoy an understated elegance in a European ambiance. There are ninety-two rooms, including eight junior and town suites; and five executive suites. All have views of either the town of Aspen or the mountain, and all have marble bathrooms with oversized tubs. The suites also have steam showers, jacuzzis, and gas fireplaces. A heated pool and indoor spa are available to soak those tired muscles.

Of course, you come here to ski, and a ski concierge will handle your equipment and can make arrangements for lessons and rentals. But don't think it ends when the lifts stop. In Aspen, that's just when life gets started. Little Nell is the place to be for *apres* ski and people-watching. Enjoy afternoon tea or a cocktail as you watch the last run come down the mountain.

The lounge restaurant specializes in Alpine-American cuisine. And the bar is one of the town's hottest nightspots. There's live jazz in the evening. And you're right in the center of town, close to the mall and all the shops, restaurants, and nightclubs of this world-class resort town. Don't leave Aspen without a drink in the lobby bar of the Hotel Jerome. Or if you want to rub shoulders with some locals, try the bar at Little Annies.

But winter is not the only time to visit Aspen. The summer offers sunshine and low humidity, with cool mountain evenings. During the summer the Aspen Music Festival attracts musicians from all over the world, where you can hear some of the Festival's students playing for free. And the off-seasons of fall and spring also have a lot to offer, often at reduced rates and without the in-season crowds. Watch the aspen trees turn gold along the mountain-sides in autumn. Or see the snow melt in a fabulous Rocky Mountain spring.

Rates: Rooms $185–$425; Suites $350–$2,900

THE LITTLE NELL
675 East Durant
Aspen, CO 81611

Phone	(970) 920-4600
Toll free	(800) 525-6200
Fax	(970) 920-4670

TRAPPER'S CABIN AT BEAVER CREEK RESORT
Avon

> Are flowers the winter's choice?
>   Is love's bed always snow?
> She seemed to hear my silent voice,
>   Not love's appeals to know.
> I never saw so sweet a face
>   As that I stood before.
> My heart has left its dwelling-place
>   And can return no more.
>
>   — "First Love" by John Clare

Here's a place where your heart can return to its old dwelling place or perhaps find a new one. Trapper's Cabin is a secluded log cabin 9,500 feet above sea level overlooking Beaver Creek. Combining impeccable service and mountain tranquility, the 3,000-square-foot cabin gives you the best of both worlds. Enjoy elegant comfort in the most private setting imaginable.

When you arrive at Beaver Creek, your baggage is taken ahead of you, delivered by snowmobile (or jeep, depending on the season) and placed in your room before you even get up the mountain. At the site, there is a cabinkeeper who serves as host, bartender, and maid to make sure that your needs are met and you are made as comfortable as possible.

Meanwhile a chef prepares your gourmet meal. You'll start out with appetizers with a Western flair, like grilled rattlesnake, smoked trout, or buffalo salami. Dinner might be such Rocky Mountain favorites as sauteed elk steaks in bourbon and wild mushroom sauce or salmon in dill butter. Dinner is served family style with fine wine followed by coffee. The chef cleans up and then prepares a heap of midnight snacks before he and the cabinkeeper depart, leaving the two of you alone for the evening.

The cabin features three bedrooms and is decorated in rustic charm, with lots of exposed beams. The dining room is hickory wood, and the living area is equipped with a player piano, a stone fireplace, a well-stocked library, board games, and a hot tub.

Breakfast will be brought to you by the chef and

cabinkeeper. Then you can plan the day's activities. In the winter you can ski right from your doorstep (lift tickets are complimentary). In the summer, you can go horseback riding or hiking. Or you can do anything you like, including nothing at all.

The cabin is reserved for one couple or group at a time.

Rates: Cabin $400–$2,000 (all inclusive)
      (based upon season)

TRAPPER'S CABIN AT BEAVER CREEK RESORT
P.O. Box 915
Avon, CO 81620

Phone   (970) 845-5788
Fax   (970) 949-4699

▬▬▬▬

Connecticut

COPPER BEECH INN
Ivoryton

> Forth, Love, and find this made,
>> Wherever she be hidden:
> Speak, Love, be not afraid,
>> But plead as thou art bidden;
> And say, that he who taught thee
>> His yearning want and pain,
> Too dearly, dearly bought thee
>> To part with thee in vain.
>
> — "Amaturus" by William Johnson Cory

Another beautiful part of the Nutmeg State is the scenic coastline along the Long Island shore. Often overshadowed by the vast Atlantic, the Connecticut shore is a famous maritime area, home port to ships bound for exotic climes.

The Copper Beech Inn is a beautiful country manor located in Ivoryton, a quaint little village near the old port town of Mystic. The Inn's guest quarters include thirteen rooms, four in the main building and nine in a renovated carriage house. Rooms on the Inn's second floor have cathedral ceilings and splendid decks. Carriage house rooms have jacuzzis. All the rooms are decorated with antiques, botanical prints, pieces from the Inn's collections of nineteenth-century art, and exquisite oriental porcelain.

The pride of the Copper Beech Inn is its rustic French restaurant. You can dine on the front porch or in one of three wood-paneled dining rooms. Fresh flowers adorn each table in the dining room, which is filled with Chippendale and Queen Anne furniture.

The Inn is owned and operated by Eldon and Sally Senner. Eldon is a gardener, and his meticulous care of

41

the grounds shows. He maintains an authentic English garden, with bulbs blooming throughout the season. Sally is an interior designer, and did most of the decorating.

Nearby attractions include Mystic Seaport, the largest maritime museum on the East Coast, which includes the ship Charles W. Morgan, one of the great nineteenth-century whaling vessels. Or you can visit the Mystic aquarium. Old Mystic Village is a charming port community filled with shops and restaurants. Of course there are countless opportunities to charter a boat for a sail on the Long Island Sound. Or you can take a long walk along the beach, and watch the sun set over the Sound, a sight so many sailors longed to see when they were far from home.

Rates: Rooms $105–$170

COPPER BEECH INN
46 Main Street
Ivoryton, CT 06442

Phone   (860) 767-0330
Fax   (860) 767-7840

MAYFLOWER INN
Washington

> Adown the pale-green glacier river floats
> A dark boat through the gloom—and whither?
> The thunder roars. But still we have each other!
> The naked lightnings in the heavens dither
> And disappear—what have we but each other?
> The boat has gone.
>
> — "On the Balcony" by D.H. Lawrence

Litchfield County is a rustic, romantic spot favored by writers, artists, media, and movie stars as a weekend retreat. Some of them even find it convenient enough to live year round. And its easy to see why the elite favor this serene yet civilized area. Lovely farmlands dot the rural thoroughfares. There are plenty of antique and specialty stores for sophisticated shoppers. And lots of great restaurants provide excellent dining in pastoral splendor.

The Mayflower Inn was built in the nineteenth-century, which makes it a relative newcomer to this historic area. The Inn is situated on twenty-eight acres of gorgeous gardens and well-tended lawns. Twenty-four guest accommodations are spread out among three separate buildings. Most of the rooms have four-poster beds and marble baths. All of them are furnished with period antiques and artwork. The restaurant and piano bar are wood paneled, as is the library. There's an outdoor heated pool, a tennis court, and fitness center. But perhaps the best attraction at the Mayflower Inn is the grand porch, filled with wicker furniture. Here is the place to sit back in a wicker loveseat with that certain someone and watch the grass grow.

If life on the porch proves to be a bit too relaxing, there's still plenty to do in the surrounding area. During the summer this area is filled with cultural events, like Tanglewood and the Norfolk Chamber Festival. In the fall, it's one of the best places for watching the resplendent colors of a New England autumn. In springtime, the countryside comes alive with lush foliage and colorful flowers.

Rates: Rooms $230–$375; Suites $395–$550

MAYFLOWER INN
Route 47
Washington, CT 06793

Phone   (203) 868-9466
Fax   (203) 868-1497

STONEHENGE INN AND RESTAURANT
Ridgefield

> No—yet still steadfast, still unchangeable,
>   Pillow'd upon my fair love's ripening breast,
> To feel for ever its soft fall and swell,
> Awake for ever in a sweet unrest,

Still, still to hear her tender-taken breath,
And so live ever—or else swoon to death.

— "Bright Star" by John Keats

New York City is just a train ride away, but you'd never know it once you've lost yourself in the bucolic surroundings of the Stonehenge Inn. Less than an hour from the excitement of the big city, you can enjoy the sylvan splendor of one of Connecticut's most exclusive suburbs.

The Stonehenge Inn is fabulously laid out, with a swan pond and rolling lawns giving way to a thicket of woods. It's conveniently located right off Route 7, yet far enough off the road that you won't hear the traffic. Instead you'll think you're visiting some stately manor house owned by someone with impeccable taste.

There are sixteen guest rooms on the ten-acre property. Make sure and get a room in the Guest House. The flagstone cocktail terrace is perfect for cooling off and winding down in the afternoon. The formal restaurant is one of the finest in an area full of great dining. In the morning, a breakfast hamper and *The New York Times* are delivered to your room.

Ridgefield is a quaint town filled with antique shops and small specialty stores, in addition to all the necessary conveniences. You can walk the tree-lined streets of this lovely town or pop over the border into New York State and enjoy a picnic at Pound Ridge Reservation. Explore the coastal towns of Westport and Norwalk just a few miles south. Or stay close to the Inn and enjoy the peaceful surroundings. Stonehenge Inn and Restaurant is a great weekend getaway from New York, or it could be the first stop on your travels north into New England.

Rates: Rooms $250; Suites $325

STONEHENGE INN AND RESTAURANT
Route 7
Ridgefield, CT 06877

Phone   (203) 438-6511
Fax   (203) 438-2478

Delaware

HOTEL DUPONT
Wilmington

> All night have the roses heard
>   The flute, violin, bassoon;
> All night has the casement jessamine stirred
>   To the dancers dancing in tune;
> Till a silence fell with the waking bird,
>   And a hush with the setting moon.
>
>   — "Song from Maud" by Alfred, Lord Tennyson

Steeped in history and tradition, the Hotel DuPont offers Old World charm along with New World convenience. Originally built by French and Italian craftsmen commissioned by Pierre DuPont, the twelve-story Italian Rennaissance building was first opened in 1913 and quickly became the great hotel of Delaware. Some of the famous guests who have stayed here include John F. Kennedy, Eleanor Roosevelt, Charles Lindbergh, Ingrid Bergman, Joe Dimaggio, and Elizabeth Taylor.

The DuPont has a unique look and style. The polished wood paneling, high ceilings, Queen Anne and Chippendale furniture, crystal chandeliers, and original artwork have all been selected to give the hotel its own classic character. The artwork in particular reflects both the historic and regional character of the hotel, which owns seven hundred original pieces by famous American artists, most of which capture the extraordinary beauty and fascinating history of the Brandywine area.

All 206 guest rooms and the ten suites have been recently renovated at a cost of $40 million, earning the hotel the coveted International Gold Key Award for design.

The public rooms in the DuPont are exquisite. The 1918 Gold Ballroom is a masterpiece in ornate, gilded beauty. The smaller du Barry room has carved peacocks and crystal chandeliers. With a capacity of more than 1,200, the Playhouse, an authentic Broadway theater, has been in operation for more than eighty years and holds the record for consecutive seasons of activity. A stage where Sarah Bernhardt, the Barrymores, Lillian Gish, Helen Hayes, Fred Astaire, and Ginger Rogers once trod is still providing a season of Broadway touring shows, children's theater, dance, and music.

There are two great restaurants in the DuPont. The elegant and formal Green Room has a musicians' gallery, Italian mosaic foyer, and towering windows. Combining the best of the new with the classics of international and regional cuisines, the Green Room features French Continental dishes. The more intimate Brandywine Room has a club-like setting, serving traditional American fare. The Lobby Lounge has a piano bar in the hotel promenade.

The DuPont offers a Romance package which includes accommodations for one night, valet parking, champagne, chocolates, flowers, and a bubble bath for $219-$259 a night, taxes and gratuities included.

Rates: Rooms $109–$229; Suites $395

HOTEL DUPONT
11th & Market Streets
Wilmington, DE 19801

Phone	(302) 594-3100
Toll free	(800) 411-9019
Fax	(302) 656-2145

District of Columbia

THE WATERGATE HOTEL
Washington, D.C.

> Your kisses close my eyes and yet you stare
> As though God struck a child with nameless fears;
> Perhaps the water glitters and discloses
> Time's chalice and its limpid useless tears.

> — "Goodbye" by Alun Lewis

To people who've never stayed at the hotel, Watergate means political scandal. But once you've spent a few nights here, Watergate only brings to mind memories of excellent food, exquisite service, and luxury accommodations in a sumptuous and convenient setting. The ambiance at The Watergate is a combination of classical elegance and contemporary sophistication. The modern architecture blends flawlessly with the period's furnishings, creating a look that is both timeless and unique.

There are 235 rooms in The Watergate, eighty-five of which are suites. The accommodations are spacious and decorated as if they were residential apartments instead of hotel rooms. The traditional decor is rounded out by gilt-framed botanical prints, and the beds are furnished with floral-print bedspreads, dust ruffles, and drapes. Make sure to ask for a suite with a view of the Potomac.

The dining rooms at The Watergate offer some of the finest cuisine in the nation's capital. Although the kitchens have just experienced a change in chefs, the food should remain consistently excellent. Enjoy a cocktail at The Potomac Lounge, where light fare and afternoon tea are also served.

As you might expect from one of Washington's finest hotels, the service is impeccable, and the amenities offer that attention to detail that the rich and powerful are accustomed to. There is twenty-four-hour room service

47

and concierge service. Nightly turndown prepares your quarters for sleeping. And in the morning you are offered a choice of seven daily newspapers. Facilities include an indoor lap pool and sundeck, jacuzzi, steam room, sauna, state-of-the-art health club offering massage and spa treatments, barber/beauty salon, gift shop, and jewelers. The Watergate shopping center offers a variety of clothing and specialty stores, as well as essentials such as a supermarket and post office.

Located between fashionable Georgetown and Foggy Bottom, and only a short cab ride from the downtown business district or the Capitol, The Watergate has an unbeatable location right on the Potomac River. The Watergate is a favorite with visiting celebrities, particularly those who are performing at the Kennedy Center next door. Recent celebrity guests include James Earl Jones, Clint Eastwood, Patrick Swayze, Carol Channing, and Richard Chamberlain.

Rates: Rooms $155–$320; Suites $395–$1,885
    (based upon season)

THE WATERGATE HOTEL
2650 Virginia Avenue, N.W.
Washington, D.C. 20037

Phone	(202) 965-2300
Toll free	(800) 424-2736
Fax	(202) 337-7915

Florida

FISHER ISLAND CLUB
Fisher Island

> How say you? Let us, O my dove,
>   Let us be unashamed of soul,
> As earth lies bare to heaven above!
>   How is it under our control
> To love or not to love?
>
>   — "Two in the Campagna"
>   by Robert Browning

Fisher Island Club is a place to be unashamed of soul, to live your romantic fantasy in a secluded island paradise that has all the luxuries of high society. This spectacular resort was originally built by descendants of William K. Vanderbilt, in the 1920s as their winter estate. Now it has been restored to its former grandeur as a world-class private club community. All this privacy and yet only three miles offshore of Miami and minutes away from lively South Beach—now that is definitely the best of both worlds.

Because Fisher Island is a private club inhabited mostly by residents, you always get the feeling that you belong someplace special. The resort offers an oceanside beach club and intimate restaurants with high-ceilinged dining rooms, and crystal chandeliers. Smaller, more intimate dining rooms have wood paneling collected from one of Napoleon's palaces. Luxurious lounges and drawing rooms overlook the swimming pool and the Atlantic Ocean. The elegant Vanderbilt Mansion offers classic cuisine. Enjoy the rustic French atmosphere of the Beach Club. Puerto Cervo is a restaurant reminiscent of the Italian Riviera. You can also relax with informal dining indoors at the Pasta Trattoria. The sporting set meets at the Golfer's Grille. Dinner theater and nightclub acts are regular entertainment at the exciting Cafe Tangier, which is mainly used for private functions.

The Club has a Mediterranean tennis center with eighteen courts, four European paddle, and four grass courts. A private mile of Atlantic Ocean beach is dotted with cabanas. Two deep-water marinas are perfect for boaters and yachters. Park lands and fitness and jogging trails allow you to exercise in the natural splendor of hibiscus, oleander, mahogany, and bougainvillea. The Links is a championship golf course. Spa Internazionale pampers residents with hydro-massage and herbal wraps in a VIP suite or one of twelve treatment rooms. There's also a beauty salon, lap pool, exercise pool, Roman waterfall whirlpool, fitness and nutritional counseling, aerobics, body sculpting, and yoga. The commercial center has shops and services overlooking the pool and marina.

Guest quarters are in circa 1925 cottages and suites on the grounds of the Vanderbilt Estate. Villa suites have one bedroom and a sitting room, marble floors, French doors, private patio, and a hot tub. Seaside villas have spectacular ocean views. The three bedroom Rosemary's cottage, once the home of Mr. and Mrs. Vanderbilt's daughter, is the prime place to stay.

If you want to visit the attractions nearby, a fleet of air-conditioned launches makes regular trips to downtown Miami and auto ferries run every fifteen minutes to Miami Beach. Visitors with their own means of transportation can use the island helipad and seaplane ramp.

Rates: Cottages $415–$1,295; Suites $525–$1,400

FISHER ISLAND CLUB
One Fisher Island Drive
Fisher Island, FL 33109

Phone	(305) 535-6000
Toll free	(800) 624-3251
Fax	(305) 535-6003

GRAND BAY HOTEL
Miami

> Time will not be ours for ever;
> He, at length, our good will sever.
> Spend not then his gifts in vain:
> Suns that set may rise again.
>
> — "Come, My Celia" by Ben Jonson

The Grand Bay is a luxurious pyramid-shaped hotel in beautiful Coconut Grove. Just minutes from downtown Miami, Coconut Grove offers all the sights and sounds of the big city, but in civilized comfort right on Biscayne Bay.

Walk into the lobby and you see two stories of soaring windows, crystal chandeliers, and sumptuous furnishings. At check-in you're greeted with that quintessential Floridian refreshment, a glass of fresh-squeezed orange juice. The floral arrangements are exquisite, featuring tropical plants and flowers. Each afternoon the lobby serves English tea accompanied by live piano music.

The hotel has 181 guest accommodations, forty-nine of which are suites. Bayfront, Unique, Bay, and Penthouse suites feature private terraces with spectacular views.

The Grand Bay is one of the few hotels in the country, if not the world, that has two first-rate restaurants. The Grand Cafe is a winner of several Golden Spoon Awards for fine dining and is considered one of Miami's best restaurants. Featuring contemporary Florida cuisine in an exotic setting of tiger lilies and orchids, the Cafe is simply superb. At the penthouse level, the art deco Regine's offers French cuisine along with a spectacular view. For lighter fare, try the Poolside Grill & Bar. Afternoon tea and cocktails are served at the Lobby Lounge. Once the sun goes down, enjoy live jazz at the CIGA Bar, and after dinner, dancing at Regine's.

When the sun rises again, there's plenty more to enjoy. Swim in the heated indoor pool or work out in the health club. Take a sail in Biscayne Bay or go shopping at

Bal Harbor. Round the clock concierge service will take care of any tickets or reservations you want.

The Grand Bay was named by *Conde Nast Traveler* as one of the top five hotels in the country and was awarded five-stars from Mobil travel guides. And it's a favorite with celebrity travelers. Luciano Pavarotti, George Bush, and Michael Jackson are just a few of the hotel's famous guests.

Rates: Rooms $205–$295; Suites $325–$1,100
    (based upon season)

GRAND BAY HOTEL
2669 South Bayshore Drive
Miami-Coconut Grove, FL 33133

Phone	(305) 858-9600
Toll free	(800) 327-2788
Fax	(305) 859-2026

▬▬▬

LITTLE PALM ISLAND
Little Torch Key

> Her South of pine and coral and coraline seas
> Her home, not mine, in the ever-freshened Keys,
> Her days, her oceanic nights, calling
> For music, for whisperings from the reefs.

> — "Farewell to Florida" by Wallace Stevens

This can be your home in the ever-freshened Keys. Little Palm Island is set on five acres of tropical hideaway that gives new meaning to the word seclusion. Located twenty-eight miles north of Key West, accessible only by water, Little Palm Island is a fifteen-minute boat ride away from Little Torch Key, but light years away from civiliza-tion. That doesn't mean it's not luxurious. In fact, all the comforts of home are here, without any of the nuisances or distractions.

Guest accommodations are in fourteen villas scattered across the island, all built on stilts to keep the floodwaters away. Inside the bamboo and thatched roof villas are twenty-eight luxury suites, with two more in the main house. The suites all have large bedrooms, living rooms, mini-bars, whirlpool baths, private sun decks, and outdoor showers. Interiors are plush and tropical, furnished in rattan and wicker. The exteriors are screened and louvered, to keep the mosquitoes and sunlight away, while allowing the tropical breezes to pass through the rooms.

The freshwater pool is fed by a waterfall and heated by solar power; its lounges are fueled by tropical drinks and snacks from the poolside Palapa Bar. An intimate beach is ringed with white sand, uncommon in the Keys. There's a small-boat harbor for guests. And the docks are a great place to watch the spectacular sunset. An exercise room and massage hut attend to your body. A dive shop will provide all you need for scuba or snorkeling. The well-stocked library has hammocks swinging outside, where you can curl up with a good book, or make bookends with someone special. Palm trees abound throughout the island—there's even one growing through the roof of the gift shop.

Of course even in paradise you have to eat. And Chef Michel Reymond serves award-winning cuisine in the Cypress Dining Room or out on the deck. The tables are set with white linen, blue-rimmed plates, and hand-blown glassware. Fresh seafood is a specialty, often imaginatively prepared. Breakfast offerings include a fresh seafood delicacy and home-baked corn and banana bread. Lunch is popular with the local yachters, salads and sandwiches served along with more adventuresome fare like raw fish marinated in lime juice. Every Wednesday the resort has a Caribbean-style barbecue out on the beach, where you can groove to a reggae band and eat fresh seafood and roast pig.

But the best part of Little Palm Island is still ahead, the gorgeous sunset and quiet, star-filled nights. This is what you've escaped civilization for—to sit out on the deck or lie in the hammock and do whatever comes naturally.

Rates: Suites $310–$685

LITTLE PALM ISLAND
2800 Overseas Highway
Little Torch Key, FL 33042

Phone   (305) 872-2524
Toll free   (800) 343-8567
Fax   (305) 872-4843

▬▬▬

SAFETY HARBOR CLUB AT UPPER CAPTIVA ISLAND
Pineland

> The lark now leaves his watery nest,
>   And climbing shakes his dewy wings.
> He takes this window for the East,
>   And to implore your light he sings --
> Awake, awake! the morn will never rise
>   Till she can dress her beauty at your eyes.
>
> — "Song" by William Davenant

Set along three miles of private beach, the Safety Harbor Club is a self-contained island colony. On one side is the Gulf of Mexico, on the other is Pine Island Sound. There are no bridges to connect the island to the mainland; water taxis take you back and forth. And once you're on the island, the only way to get around is by bicycle or golf cart. Of course you can go on foot, and the island is small enough that you can get around easily without conveyance.

This is a tropical paradise with isolated white sand beaches, world renowned shelling, subtropical foliage, and trees. It's a bird-watcher's haven and great for saltwater fishing. Snook and dolphin cavort in the water nearby. The beach is pristine, with the shell-pink sand the Gulf Coast is famous for. Accommodations are in townhouses, duplexes, and single cottages, designed for privacy and protected by lush foliage. Each guest quarter has a full kitchen, laundry facilities, phone, cable television, and large living area.

The clubhouse offers a freshwater swimming pool. There are also tennis courts. And bird watchers will love the observation tower for keeping an eye on the migratory birds. There are three small restaurants and a general store if you'd prefer to eat in.

The Safety Harbor Club doesn't offer all the amenities of a full resort. But that's precisely why some people prefer it. There's less pressure to keep busy, and you're left to your own devices. While there's plenty to do, you might prefer doing nothing at all. Or doing something the two of you don't need any assistance with.

Rates: Townhouses and Single-Family Homes
$1,000–$2,500 weekly (based upon season)

SAFETY HARBOR CLUB AT UPPER CAPTIVA ISLAND
P.O. Box 2276
Pineland, FL 33945

Phone   (941) 472-1056
Fax   (941) 472-1381

VILLA DE ESPANA (PRIVATE RESIDENCE)
Miami

> What is love? 'Tis not hereafter;
> Present mirth hath present laughter;
> What's to come is still unsure:
> In delay there lies no plenty;
> Then come kiss me, sweet and twenty,
> Youth's a stuff will not endure.
>
> — *Twelfth Night* by William Shakespeare

Youth may not endure, but love can be prolonged by a romantic hideaway in a private residence or even in a private yacht.

Enjoy a once-in-a-lifetime holiday by renting a mansion on Millionaire's Row in Miami Beach. One offering is a $3.9 million waterfront mansion featuring six bedrooms, seven and a half baths, a fully equipped weight room, billiard room, Olympic swimming pool, whirlpool spas, a wet bar, tennis court, deep-water dockage for your yacht, and much more. Minutes from South Beach, Bal Harbor, and all the scenes and attractions of lively Miami, this stately pleasure dome includes full amenities and staff. Doesn't that sound like the ultimate luxury vacation?

Rates: House $1,000 (6 night, 7 day minimum) $30,000 (a month)

Contact: David Ross   (305) 576-5515
                       (305) 868-7567

████

Georgia

PRESIDENTS' QUARTERS
Savannah

> I cried for madder music and for stronger wine,
> But when the feast is finished and the lamps expire,
> Then falls thy shadow, Cynara the night is thine.
>
> — "Non Sum Qualis Eram Bonae Sub Regno
> Cynarae" by Ernest Dowson

If you've read *Midnight in the Garden of Good and Evil* (or even just heard about it), you know that Savannah is the place for madder music and stronger wine. Ever since John Berendt's steamy and hilarious bestseller put Savannah on the map, this charming southern city has been opening its doors for wandering romantics from all over the world.

Of the many fine inns and bed and breakfasts in Savannah, the Presidents' Quarters is the best. There are only sixteen rooms in this pair of Greek Revival brick townhouses, but seven of them are suites, and four of those are on the concierge level. Even if you don't go for the concierge level, you'll still enjoy impeccable, personalized treatment. All guests receive a basket of fruit, a bottle of wine, and nightly turndown service with personalized chocolate mints on their pillows, and a glass of port or sherry before bed. Linens, towels, and bathrobes are also personalized, making you feel as if you were a president yourself.

The Presidents' Quarters earned its name by being host to twenty presidents since 1885. The famous exterior of the Quarters was also used in the famous "Roots" television miniseries. All of the rooms have a view, and six of them are spectacular, looking out over Oglethorpe Square in the heart of Savannah's historic district. Every room has a gas log fireplace, jacuzzi bathtub, brass appointments, ceiling fans, and balconies. The honeymoon suites have loft bedrooms and king-sized beds.

There is no restaurant in the Presidents' Quarters, but continental breakfast is served every morning, and there are a host of fine restaurants nearby. The Quarters also serves room service twenty-four hours a day from a simple menu. Afternoon tea is provided daily in the lobby, or you can take it in the private enclosed courtyard by the pool. And the inn is only a twenty minute drive from Savannah Beach.

The Presidents' Quarters is a favorite with celebrities who are staying in Savannah. Karl Malden spent a month there. Bruce and Andrea Dern spent nearly as long. Other guests have included Joanna Cassidy and President Phillip Hillary of Ireland.

Rates: Rooms $117–$130; Suites $140–$167

PRESIDENTS' QUARTERS
225 East President Street
Savannah, GA 31401

Phone	(912) 233-1600
Toll free	(800) 233-1776
Fax	(912) 238-0849

RITZ-CARLTON BUCKHEAD
Atlanta

> Were you not still my hunger's rarest food,
> And water ever to my wildest thirst,
> I would desert you—think not but I would!—
> And seek another as I sought you first.
>
> — "Oh, Think Not I Am Faithful to a Vow!"
> by Edna St. Vincent Millay

A first-class hotel, which is beginning to be recognized as one of the finest in the country, Ritz-Carlton Buckhead is about fifteen minutes from downtown Atlanta, and convenient to Lenox Square and Phipps Plaza.

The lobby entrance welcomes you into a small foyer appointed with Honduras mahogany moldings and

African Sappele hardwood paneling. Italian Botticino classic white marble with inlaid continental mahogany from Tennessee are the backdrop to antique Persian carpets and authentic antiques. Inside the reception lobby, exquisitely cut crystal chandeliers and wall sconces sparkle. All the public areas of the hotel are decorated with museum quality eighteenth- and nineteenth-century European and American art works.

The Dining Room is one of Atlanta's best restaurants. The atmosphere is one of a grand residence, with silk-upholstered seating, elegantly appointed tables, museum quality art, and classical music playing softly in the background. Chef Guenter Seeger creates his menu daily to ensure the freshest and finest ingredients. A master sommelier is on hand to help you with your wine selection. The Cafe also offers great food, including a spectacular Sunday brunch. The Lobby Lounge is an elegant yet relaxing place for afternoon tea, evening cocktails, and live piano music on the Steinway. Expresso's is the hotel's popular deli, offering take-out or casual dining inside or out on the patio.

The Ritz-Carlton Club features exclusive key access, a private lounge, and the personalized service of an expertly trained concierge staff. Upon joining the club, you are ensured the ultimate in privacy, luxury, and service, including five complimentary food presentations daily, from breakfast to turn-down treats.

The Ritz-Carlton Buckhead has received AAA's Five Diamond Award for ten consecutive years. It has also won Mobil's Four Star Award, in addition to numerous other kudos from professional travel experts.

Rates: Rooms $195–$260; Suites $365–$1,050

RITZ-CARLTON BUCKHEAD
3434 Peachtree Road NE
Atlanta, GA 30326

Phone	(404) 237-2700
Toll free	(800) 241-3333
Fax	(404) 239-0078

THE CLOISTER
Sea Island

> If things on earth may be to heaven resembled,
> It must be love, pure, constant, undissembled.
> But if to sin by chance the charmer press,
> Forgive, O Lord, forgive our trespasses.
>
> — "And Forgive Us Our Trespasses" by Aphra Behn

This classic vacation colony is set on a 10,000-acre island of beachfront solitude connected to St. Simons Island by a causeway. Experienced travelers consistently rate The Cloister as one of the best resorts in the country. The buildings are designed in Mediterranean style offering 262 rooms surrounded by stunning gardens and set along a five mile beach.

The Cloister has some of the best golfing in the world. The two golf courses which are equal to fifty-four holes, are set on historic Retreat Plantation along the majestic Avenue of Oaks. There are seventeen clay tennis courts which include one automated court for private warmups and practice. Every morning there's a Seaside Morning Stretch and Morning Beach Walk. Other activities include horseback riding, a fitness center, freshwater swimming pools, and shooting ranges. The beach club provides a variety of water sports. Sailing and fishing charters are offered at the resort's marina.

Throughout your stay, your own table is reserved for you, adorned with fresh flowers. Friday nights feature a spectacular outdoor plantation supper. And every night The Cloister provides a variety of live music. Big bands make The Cloister one of America's top destinations for ballroom dancers. You can dance to the music before and after dinner. The main dining room serves six-course dinners accompanied by live music. The Beach Club has indoor and outdoor breakfast and lunch buffets, and seafood dinner buffets.

Just because it's called The Cloister doesn't mean you have to live like a monk. The staff is attentive to the needs of romantic couples, and they specialize in welcoming honeymooners and anniversary celebrants.

Honeymoon packages include amenities such as dancing, champagne welcome, breakfast in bed, and a weekly honeymooner party.

Rates: Rooms $252–$476; Suites $302–$476 (based upon season) (all meals included)

THE CLOISTER
100 Hudson Place
Sea Island, GA 31561

Phone   (912) 638-3611
Toll free   (800) 732-4752
Fax   (912) 638-5159

Hawaii

HOTEL HANA MAUI
Hana Maui

> Whether in the bringing of the flowers or of the food
> She offers plenty, and is part of plenty,
> And whether I see her stooping, or leaning with the
>   flowers,
> What she does is ages old, and she is not simply,
> No, but lovely in that way.
>
> — "Part of Plenty" by Bernard Spencer

The Hotel Hana Maui isn't easy to get to, and that's part of its charm. Accessible only by small plane or a three-hour jeep drive, guests are assured the ultimate in peace, quiet, and privacy.

This tropical island sanctuary offers the ultimate in luxurious seclusion. Guest quarters are seventy-two rooms and suites in one-story cottages situated throughout the property. Each room has a private veranda with views of Hana Bay, the Pacific Ocean, or the lush surrounding gardens. The local staff serves you with warmth, friendliness, and a knowledge of the island. Flowers, both wild and cultivated, abound throughout the property.

If you feel like being social, the main building houses a restaurant, bar, library, and gift shop. The dining room has a high open-beam ceiling and covered outdoor patio, serving American specialties with an Oriental flavor. A grilled lunch is usually served on the beach, which is eaten together with other guests or else in a private picnic. Every Friday night there's a luau on the beach. Evening entertainment is offered in both the bar and dining room. The bar has a wood-burning fireplace, while the dining room has a spectacular skylight.

The open air clubhouse is furnished in bamboo and

rattan. A beautifully landscaped courtyard in the center comes complete with a lilypond. The resort is a working ranch and features horseback riding, trail rides, and even overnight treks. Jeep tours of the island are available. And while the property is not directly on a sandy beach, there is a shuttle to take you to one nearby. Also available are two tennis courts, cycling, a practice golf course, and hiking trails. Snorkeling and scuba diving are superb in the crystalline waters.

Hana Maui is a wonderful place for romance. Honeymoon and anniversaries are a specialty here, and the staff is ready to indulge your every whim, satisfy your pleasures, or simply leave you alone. Caroline Kennedy spent her honeymoon here. And celebrities such as Kenny Rogers and Eddie Albert, and basketball great Kareem Abdul-Jabbar are frequent visitors. Charles Lindbergh came to the Hana coast to retire and is buried nearby.

Rates: Rooms $395; Suites $450–$795

HOTEL HANA MAUI
P.O. Box 8
Hana Maui, HI 96713

Phone   (808) 248-8211
Fax   (808) 248-7202

■

KAPALUA BAY HOTEL & VILLAS
Kapalua-Maui

> My beloved is mine and I am his,
>   he pastures his flock among the lilies.
> Until the day breathes
>   and the shadows flee,
> turn, my beloved, be like a gazelle,
>   or a young stag upon rugged mountains.
>
>   — "Song of Solomon, Chapter Two" attributed to
>   King Solomon

This is another spectacular place to stay on the gorgeous island of Maui. Situated in the middle of a private pineapple plantation, Kapalua is nestled on 750 acres of lush grounds along Maui's northwest coast.

Kapalua specializes in combining elegant service with tropical serenity. Everything is built on a human scale, so it doesn't attempt to compete with the surrounding beauty. The hotel itself is so well-integrated into the landscape that you'd never know from looking at it that there are 194 rooms and three suites. The structure is open to allow for breezes and unobstructed views. Upon arrival, you'll receive a traditional lei in the lobby, which provides a sweeping vista of the Pacific and neighboring islands. Spacious rooms feature his and her vanities and private lanais, which are patios. The room's mini-bars are stocked with such delicacies as Maui potato chips, Swiss chocolates, champagne, and caviar. If you don't want to, you'll never have to leave your room.

But if you do decide to explore, there's plenty to do and see. The Garden Restaurant features casual dining in a setting of flowering waterways and lava rock gardens. A short walk down the beach path and you're at the Bay Club, a gourmet restaurant set on a lava promontory overlooking the Pacific. This is an award-winning restaurant specializing in continental cuisine, and decorated with original pastel paintings for romantic ambiance. While lounging at the butterfly-shaped swimming pool, you can enjoy a complimentary serving of pineapple, served ice-cold from a roving cart. Meal service is available at the Pool Terrace, where fresh-catch favorites like Mahi-Mahi are served al fresco.

And there's plenty of sporting activities to keep you busy. Two championship eighteen-hole golf courses offer some of the most spectacular settings in the world. Complete beach facilities include windsurfing, sailing, and scuba diving. Of course you can just lay back on the sand or take a romantic walk on the beach.

For guests who prefer the informal privacy of a vacation home, Kapalua offers spacious villas. Tucked away in richly landscaped clusters, the Golf, Ridge, and Bay villas offer all the luxury of a private home and include recreational facilities. Villas are available to rent by the day, week, or month.

The list of celebrity guests at the Kapalua reads like a who's who, ranging alphabetically from Loni Anderson to Oprah Winfrey and just about everyone in between. *Lifestyles of the Rich and Famous* has repeatedly ranked Kapalua among the world's best resorts. In ancient Hawaiian, Kapalua means "arms embracing the sea." It's also the perfect spot for other kinds of embracing.

Rates: Rooms and Villas $200–$495; Suites $760-$1,260

KAPALUA BAY HOTEL & VILLAS
1 Bay Drive
Kapalua-Maui, HI 96761

Phone	(808) 669-5656
Toll free	(800) 367-8000
Fax	(808) 669-4694

KONA VILLAGE RESORT
Kaupulehu-Kona

> O hurry to the ragged wood, for there
> I will drive all those lovers out and cry—
> O my share of the world, O yellow hair!
> No one has ever loved but you and I.
>
> — "The Ragged Wood" by W. B. Yeats

At the foot of Mt. Hualalai, along a pristine stretch of natural sandy beach, an authentic Polynesian village lies nestled between the fingers of a centuries-old lava flow. This could be a native village on Fiji or Samoa, but instead you're on the big island of Hawaii. Secluded from the rest of the world by thousands of undeveloped acres, Kona Village is a tropical island arcadia. There are no telephones, no radios, and no televisions. Just gorgeous beach and sun and privacy. And the two of you, alone together in a world of your own.

Kona Village combines edenic privacy with luxurious comfort. The 125 guest accommodations are in thatched bungalows, authentic "hales" surrounding peaceful lagoons, tropical gardens, or the town of Kaupulehu's beautiful beach. Some of the huts are even built on stilts to keep above the rising tides and rainfloods. There is no air conditioning—and no need for it—as cool tropical breezes waft through the well-ventilated cottages.

The tropical island atmosphere is reflected in exquisite details. Torches light the property at night, the hotel office resembles a jungle trading post, and the dining room is a replica of a New Hebrides longhouse. Guided nature hikes and historical tours are available. You can explore the ancient shelter caves or learn about traditional Hawaiian arts and crafts. Tennis, sailing, snorkeling, deep-sea fishing, and scuba diving are also available.

Once you visit Kona Village, you'll want to come back. In fact, half of Kona's guests return to the resort. One of the reasons visitors are so satisfied is that the price is all-inclusive; there are no hidden charges. What you're quoted is what it will cost. And it's the perfect place for a recharge. Robert Waterman, author of *In Search of Excellence,* highlighted Kona Village in his recent book *The Renewal Factor.* Drawing on his own frequent visits to the village, Waterman wrote that the management "knows how to retain the best of the past and still change with the times. It's a fine example of renewal."

Whether you need renewal, or you're starting fresh, this is the place to do it. Kona Village is a great place for a romantic wedding on the beach at sunset, with the soft hum of guitars and the sweet fragrance of pikaki and maile filling the air. They offer four- and seven-night honeymoon packages, which can include all wedding arrangements, down to the photographer. Guests are called to weddings with the traditional blowing of the conch shell. The bride and groom are presented with traditional maile and pikake wedding leis. The Honeymoon packages range from $2,315 for four nights or $3,935 for seven nights. Specific units can be reserved only for a minimum seven-night stay.

Rates: Bungalows $395–$680 (all inclusive)

KONA VILLAGE RESORT
P.O. Box 1299
Kaupulehu-Kona, HI 96745

Phone	(808) 325-5555
Toll free	(800) 367-5290
Fax	(808) 325-5124

Illinois

SIERRA HOTEL RAILWAY
Chicago

> O the engineer's joys! To go with a locomotive!
> To hear the hiss of steam, the merry shriek, the steam-
> whistle,
>   the laughing locomotive!
> To push with resistless way and speed off in the
> distance.
>
> — "A Song of Joys" by Walt Whitman

If you wish to share the engineer's joys (but don't want any of his responsibilities), you can rent your own rail car. The Sierra Hotel features private deluxe rail cruising. With private bedrooms and three lounge areas, you can move around as the train car travels through scenic locales. A special dome level has a glass-ceiling viewing area so you can take in the sights. This is also where meals prepared on board are served. You can also relax in the spacious main lounge or in the cocktail lounge located on the lower level, underneath the dome.

Rates: To charter one rail car $3,000–$5,000
    (all meals included)

SIERRA HOTEL RAILWAY
77 West Wacker Drive, 17th Floor
Chicago, IL 60601

Phone   (312) 326-7796
Fax   (312) 326-7778

THE RITZ-CARLTON
Chicago

> She opened her eyes, and green
> They shone, clear like flowers undone
> For the first time, now for the first time seen.

— "Green" by D.H. Lawrence

You can love till dawn in the Windy City, a place second to none for excitement and nightlife. Located right on the Magnificent Mile at Water Tower Place, The Ritz-Carlton offers great location, timeless surroundings, exemplary guest facilities, and unparalleled service.

Thoughtful details in every guest room include luxurious marble bathrooms equipped with full length cotton robes and hair dryers so you can travel light. Mini-bars and in-room safes provide convenience and safety. Twenty-four hour valet and room service are available to fulfill your every need. Of the 431 oversized guest rooms, eighty-two are suites. Among them, Four Seasons Executive Suites offer a separate parlor. A baby grand piano, dining room, and study distinguish the two-level State Suite. And the Anniversary Suites are intimate accommodations with spectacular city views. Within these suites the living areas and bedrooms are separated by French doors and the bathrooms feature oversized tubs and floor-to-ceiling windows overlooking the city.

Dining at The Ritz-Carlton offers a variety of enticing choices. French contemporary cuisine is served amidst a posh setting of crystal chandeliers and cozy banquettes in the Dining Room. The restaurant is regarded as one of Chicago's finest, and Chef Sarah Stegner and Pastry Chef Sebastien Canonne are among the Windy City's brightest culinary stars. The Cafe provides a casual setting for breakfast, lunch, dinner, and late-night dining. The Greenhouse serves a light luncheon buffet, traditional English afternoon tea, and evening cocktails in an atrium setting with a striking view of Chicago's lake front. Evening piano music sets a graceful tone for a romantic night in the heart of the city. The Trianon also provides an intimate atmosphere for cocktails.

The Ritz-Carlton specializes in catering to pet owners,

offering a full range of pet-friendly accommodations and services like a gourmet pet room service menu and on-premise kennel and dog walking service. Now you don't have to leave Fido or Kitty behind on your romantic getaway.

The Ritz-Carlton offers a variety of special packages, including the Romantic Weekend. The package includes welcome cocktails at the Bar or Greenhouse; accommodations in the quiet luxury of an elegant guest room, where you'll enjoy complimentary champagne accompanied by chocolate-dipped strawberries; full American breakfast for two; and use of the Carlton Club and Spa. What you do with the rest of your time is up to you.

Rates: Rooms $290–$305; Suites $330–$795

THE RITZ-CARLTON
160 East Pearson Street
Chicago, IL 60611

Phone	(312) 266-1000
Toll free	(800) 332-3442
Fax	(312) 266-1194

Indiana

THE CANTERBURY HOTEL
Indianapolis

> Great cheer our host gave us, every one,
> And to the supper set us all anon
> Strong was the wine and pleasant to each guest.
>
> — *The Canterbury Tales* by Geoffrey Chaucer

Travel back to the romantic past in The Canterbury Hotel. This national historic landmark was built in 1928 and has retained much of its Jazz Age splendor without sacrificing modern comforts. The rooms are comfortable and luxurious, decorated with Chippendale furniture and four-poster beds decked in Irish linen. The bathrooms are constructed of fine marble with elegant fittings. A mahogany-paneled sitting room off of the lobby has a carved wooden fireplace and exquisite library, the perfect place to relax and converse. The lobby itself is a work of art, furnished with antiques and offering a stately yet comfortable ambiance.

Arriving in Indianapolis, you can have The Canterbury's Mercedes limousine pick you up at the airport and take you to the hotel. The atmosphere is "veddy" British, with afternoon tea served in the atrium and a focus on personal service.

The Restaurant at Canterbury features American and Continental fare. Candlelight dining, wood paneling, and a hunting theme decor add to the romantic atmosphere along with the superb cuisine. After dinner at the Restaurant at Canterbury, you can take a horse-drawn carriage through downtown Indianapolis, or enjoy a quiet cocktail in the hotel's lounge.

The location can't be beat. The Canterbury is close to the train station, convention center, Monument Circle, and Hoosier Dome. A Canterbury Honeymoon package includes champagne and strawberries on arrival and continental breakfast the next morning.

Rates: Rooms $125–$225; Suites $275–$1,200

THE CANTERBURY HOTEL
123 South Illinois Street
Indianapolis, IN 46225

Phone	(317) 634-3000
Toll free	(800) 538-8186
Fax	(317) 685-2519

Kentucky

THE SEELBACH HOTEL
Louisville

> By the next autumn she was gay again, gay as ever. She had a debut after the Armistice, and in February she was presumably engaged to a man from New Orleans. In June she married Tom Buchanan of Chicago, with more pomp and circumstance than Louisville had ever known before.
>
> — *The Great Gatsby* by F. Scott Fitzgerald

The Seelbach Hotel had already been famous for twenty years before Fitzgerald immortalized it in his great novel. The hotel was built in 1905 by brothers Louis and Otto Seelbach, who wanted to bring a grand hotel to this Ohio River city. The brothers brought marble from Italy and Switzerland for the entrance and decorated the lobby with murals depicting Kentucky's pioneer days. The lobby is nothing less than spectacular, with a flowing grand stairway, rich with the original brass, marble, and mahogany the Seelbachs were justly proud of.

The hotel has 323 rooms decorated in eighteenth-century style, complete with armoires, four-poster beds, marble baths, and various pieces of mahogany furniture, including traditional writing tables. Concierge-class accommodations offer a special level of personal service and luxury, including a private lounge with beverages and complimentary hors d'oeuvres.

The renowned Oakroom Restaurant offers refined service and an eclectic menu created by some of the finest chefs in the region. The exquisite American cuisine features both seasonal and classic entrees. A luxurious setting of burnished oak and detailed hand carvings, the Oakroom is stately yet intimate. The tables are comfortably set apart for intimate dining and private conversation. For romantic entertainment, enjoy piano jazz in the Old Seelbach Bar, which *Esquire* rated as one of the best bars in the South.

The hotel is a few short blocks from Louisville's riverfront and the world's largest floating fountain, the Falls Fountain, where computerized jets propel water into a 375-foot-high fleur-de-lis pattern, the symbol of Louisville. Anchored nearby is the Belle of Louisville, the oldest operating riverboat in the United States. A number of presidents have stayed at The Seelbach: William Howard Taft, Woodrow Wilson, Franklin Roosevelt, Harry Truman, John Kennedy, and Lyndon Johnson.

If you'd like to visit The Seelbach during Kentucky Derby week, make your reservations way, way in advance. Sorry, but reservations are no longer taken for Daisy Buchanan's wedding...

Rates: Rooms $132–$180; Suites $210–$510

THE SEELBACH HOTEL
500 Fourth Avenue
Louisville, KY 40202

Phone	(502) 585-3200
Toll free	(800) 333-3399
Fax	(502) 585-9239

Louisiana

BOURBON ORLEANS HOTEL
New Orleans

> Nothing remains but desire, and desire comes howling
> down Elysian Fields like a mistral.
>
> — *The Moviegoer* by Walker Percy

Desire in all its various guises finds a home here in New
Orleans. They even named a streetcar after it. And any
visitor to the Crescent City knows that the heart of this
throbbing city is the French Quarter. The Bourbon
Orleans Hotel is located right in the center of the French
Quarter, offering convenience to that neighborhood's
lively street scene and great restaurants. Yet it is away
from the "hustle and bustle" of Bourbon Street.

The Bourbon Orleans dates back to 1817, when the
Orleans Ballroom was built by John Davis to cater to the
city's insatiable love for dancing and entertainment.
Masquerade balls, carnival celebrations, and even the
notorious Quadroon balls—in which wealthy Creole gen-
tlemen selected their mistresses—were held there. In
1881, the building was sold to the Sisters of the Holy
Family, becoming the first African American convent in
the country.

Now it's anything but a convent. The Bourbon
Orleans has been completely restored to its original state
of Old World charm and sophistication. The lobby is decorated with fourteen-foot columns with gold leaf accents.
Intricate moldings, painted crests, and garlands add to
the baroque ambiance. The ceiling is covered with a
fresco of heavenly skies and cherubs.

The hotel has 211 rooms, fifty of which are bilevel
suites with the bedrooms upstairs. A few of these suites
offer balconies looking out onto the street where you can
enjoy your morning chickory coffee, or watch the

fascinating street traffic in the evening. All the rooms have a state-of-the-art video system, so you can choose from a wide variety of classic films and new releases in the privacy and comfort of your own room. You can also order room service through the interactive television system. Bathrooms are decorated with Italian marble and have their own telephones.

The public spaces are decorated with chandeliers, Oriental rugs, and marble floors. The Cafe Lafayette offers first class New Orleans cuisine. The lobby bar serves hors d'oeuvres at cocktail hour. A great place to chill out is the hotel pool, away from the sometimes overwhelming excitement of this great city. For a relatively peaceful stay in New Orleans, you might want to avoid the mob scenes at Mardi Gras and the Jazz Festival. Also, the week between Christmas and the New Year can get pretty boisterous with Sugar Bowl fans.

Rates: Rooms $115–$135; Suites $165–$325
    (based upon season)

BOURBON ORLEANS HOTEL
717 Orleans Street
New Orleans, LA 70116

Phone	(504) 523-2222
Toll free	(800) 521-5338
Fax	(504) 525-8166

THE LAFAYETTE HOTEL
New Orleans

> Oh, the first flowers—what a scent they have!
> And what a charm breathes in the murmuring
> Of the first yes that comes from lips you love!
>
> — "Nevermore" by Paul Verlaine

On mornings in New Orleans you can smell the delicate fragrance of magnolia blossoms and jasmine, the fresh scent of boiling coffee and frying beignets, the smells of a city coming awake. And if you stay at The Lafayette, you can bask in those New Orleans mornings because you got a pleasant sleep the night before, often a rarity in this city that rarely sleeps.

The Lafayette is located on St. Charles Avenue, right on the streetcar line and only a few blocks from the French Quarter. It's a little quieter than hotels in the Quarter itself, but you don't have to sacrifice convenience. Overlooking Lafayette Square right in the heart of the city, The Lafayette is a favorite with frequent visitors to the Big Easy. The hotel is within walking distance of the Superdome, the historical arts and warehouse districts, and the convention center. And it's an easy streetcar ride to Audubon Park, Tulane University, and the antebellum houses of the Garden District.

The architecture of The Lafayette Hotel features the French doors and wrought-iron balconies characteristic of New Orleans' turn of the century buildings. Inside the hotel, the foyer shows off a gleaming Italian marble floor, exquisite wood moldings, an English carpet, and a French polished mahogany front desk. Upstairs are twenty-two rooms and twenty-two suites. Each guest quarter is individually decorated with English botanical prints and classic furnishings. The marble baths have brass fixtures. The suites come complete with their own wet bars; some have four-poster beds and whirlpool baths.

Mike's on the Avenue, located in the hotel, is one of the hottest restaurants in New Orleans. For those weary of the rich dishes of Creole cuisine, this is an inspired departure. Mike Fennelly was the chef at the famous

Santacafe in Santa Fe, and his specialty is East-meets-Southwest.

All in all, The Lafayette is a blend of new and old, of tried and true New Orleans, with a few funky twists. It's worth a try, particularly for those who think they have seen it all in this city of surprises. And if you come here with someone you'd like to get to know better or someone you want to meet all over again, then this is the peaceful alternative.

Rates: Rooms $119–$350; Suites $189–$650

THE LAFAYETTE HOTEL
600 St. Charles Avenue
New Orleans, LA 70130

Phone   (504) 524-4441
Toll free   (800) 733-4754
Fax   (504) 523-7327

Maine

BLACK POINT INN
Prouts Neck

> Trust me, I mind not, though Life lours,
>   The bringing me here; nay bring me here again!
>   I am just the same as when
> Our days were a joy, and our paths through flowers.

— "After a Journey" by Thomas Hardy

Rocky, windswept coastline and some of the most beautiful unspoiled scenery in the United States. Fresh lobsters and other local seafood. The salty sea air, the tang of Yankee wit. That's what you'll find here at some of the resorts and inns in Maine. They are a little more austere than their brethren in other parts of the country. But that doesn't mean they're lacking in romance.

Located only twenty minutes from Portland, Maine's largest city, the Black Point Inn is a secluded spot on the peninsula of Prout's Neck. The peninsula itself is a small town, and it abounds in quaint, homey atmosphere. Many of the visitors who return to Black Point year after year consider themselves residents. The village has a post office and general store where locals gather to shop and converse.

The Inn has eighty rooms, most of which have spectacular views. There's a fireplace in the lobby, which burns year round, for even summer evenings can get somewhat chilly. For swimming you have two options, the outdoor saltwater pool or the indoor freshwater pool. There are deep-sea fishing charters, bike rentals, and sailing available. And the beautiful beach is always there for sunbathing, picnics, bird watching, long walks, or even swimming, if you're brave enough. Guests have full run of the eighteen-hole golf course and fourteen tennis courts at the nearby Prout's Neck Country Club. The

Inn's cocktail lounge offers live music six nights a week, with a hot combo on weekends. The restaurant serves fantastic food, featuring local seafood specialties caught that day, along with great desserts. Afternoon tea is served in summer. Dining is elegant, with finger bowl service and piano music. Jackets and ties are required. Once the governor of Connecticut was asked to leave the Meeting Room lounge because he wasn't wearing a tie. "But I'm the governor of Connecticut," he protested. "You're not in Connecticut now," he was told.

Lunch is served buffet-style by the pool, or you can opt for a picnic on the beach. During the day visit the famous Portland Lighthouse at Cape Elizabeth. Nearby Portland's Museum of Art features the world's largest collection of paintings by Winslow Homer, whose studio is within walking distance of the Inn. For shoppers, Portland has many quaint stores, and L.L. Bean is less than a half hour away.

Rates: Rooms $250–$370; Suites $280–$400
(3 night minimum) (based upon season)

BLACK POINT INN
510 Black Point Road
Prouts Neck, ME 04074

Phone	(207) 883-4126
Toll free	(800) 258-0003
Fax	(207) 883-9976

WHITE BARN INN
Kennebunkport

> Thus in the winter stands the lonely tree,
> Nor knows what birds have vanished one by one,
> Yet knows its boughs more silent than before:
> I cannot say what loves have come and gone,
> I only know that summer sang in me
> A little while, that in me sings no more.
>
> — "What Lips My Lips Have Kissed"
>   by Edna St. Vincent Millay

Now that Kennebunkport no longer serves as the summer White House, the crowds have thinned out a bit, and the town is no longer overrun by journalists and other nuisances. Kennebunkport can go back to being a charming coastal Maine town, which was why people like George Bush have been going there for so long. And if you don't happen to own a summer house here, the place to stay is the White Barn Inn.

For over a century and a half, the White Barn Inn has been a special place for those who appreciate traditional service, exquisite food, and comfortable lodging. The candlelit dining room is built in a converted barn with wood interior walls, exposed rafters, and lots of rustic antique decorations. An ornate stained glass window stands behind the brass bar. Candles light the piano bar. Entrées in the dining room might include bacon wrapped sea scallops in maple mustard cream or oven roasted quail. Try the steamed Maine lobster on fresh fettucine with carrots and ginger in a spicy honey and sherry vinegar sauce. The second dining room is an attached barn room with an exquisite floral display. And there's a third dining room featuring classical guitar music. The Bushes and other local gentry are frequent visitors to the Inn's dining rooms.

All the guest rooms are furnished with New England period pieces. The Fireplace Suites in the Carriage House have working fireplaces, whirlpool baths, and four-poster beds. Each of the four rooms in the Gate House has an entry porch and sleigh bed. Rooms in the seven-suite Carriage House have four-poster beds, sitting areas, and marble bathrooms with whirlpools.

The Inn is just a five-minute walk to the town of Kennebunkport, where you will find a charming variety of shops, antique stores, and galleries. Nearby are some of the finest beaches in Maine. Pick wild blueberries in August at Blueberry Plains in West Kennebunk. Or visit Walker's Point, the Bush summer home.

The Kennebunkport Inn offers special midweek romantic getaways starting at $160, as well as several holiday and off-season packages.

Rates: Rooms $150–$302; Suites $320–$450
        (based upon season)

WHITE BARN INN
P.O. Box 560C
Kennebunkport, ME 04046

Phone   (207) 967-2321
Fax   (207) 967-1100

Maryland

HARBOR COURT
Baltimore

> The city now doth, like a garment, wear
> The beauty of the morning; silent, bare,
> Ships, towers, domes, theatres, and temples lie
> Open to the fields, and to the sky;
> All bright and glittering in the smokeless air.
>
> — "Composed upon Westminster Bridge"
>   by William Wordsworth

If you don't think Baltimore is a beautiful, romantic city, you haven't been there recently. The Inner Harbor, Camden Yards, and a host of other downtown attractions have turned Baltimore from a frog into a prince. And Harbor Court is right in the middle of it all, across the street from the Inner Harbor and a short jaunt from just about everything else in town.

Walking into the Harbor Court, the first thing to strike you is the breathtaking lobby, with its long, curving staircase, oak paneling, and marble floors. This kind of elegant detail is replicated throughout the hotel, particularly in the individually and elegantly decorated suites and private dining rooms.

The restaurants are similarly superb. Cafe Brighton serves breakfast, lunch, and dinner, as well as afternoon tea. Understated elegance is the theme of this room, with sunny charm, a crystal chandelier, and a baroque painted ceiling. One reviewer described Cafe Brighton as "Marie Antoinette playing shepherdess." Hampton's is one of the premier restaurants of Baltimore. Serving only dinner and Sunday brunch, this gourmet dining establishment has a stunning panoramic view of the harbor. Entrées like veal chop in madeira with escargots or blackened buffalo with mushroom and shallot marmalade have impressed food and travel experts. Enhancing the inventive menu is a wine list that is simply tremendous. You can also enjoy cocktails at the Explorer's Lounge, filled with the mementos of nineteenth-century travelers. The lounge serves drinks and light meals, and features live music in the evenings.

Activities include a rooftop health club, providing the latest innovations in fitness and exercise. The equipment is all top of the line, and there's an indoor lap pool, specially designed aerobics room, saunas, a whirlpool, training bed, racquetball, and tennis courts.

Rates: Rooms $160–$220; Suites $350–$2,000

HARBOR COURT
550 Light Street
Baltimore, MD 21202

Phone	(410) 234-0550
Toll free	(800) 824-0076
Fax	(410) 659-5925

THE INN AT PERRY CABIN
St. Michaels

> The hour of the waning of love has beset us,
> And weary and worn are our sad souls now;
> Let us part, ere the season of passion forget us,
> With a kiss and a tear on thy drooping brow.
>
> — "The Falling of the Leaves" by W. B. Yeats

If you like the Laura Ashley look, you'll love The Inn at Perry Cabin. Owned by Sir Bernard Ashley, chairman of Laura Ashley, the Inn is decorated with the latest of this exquisite designer line. But it's more than just a fabric pattern, the Inn has the elegant and historic charm of an English country house, maintained by an accommodating old friend.

Situated on the peaceful, civilized, and serenely beautiful eastern shore of Maryland, this 1820 Greek Revival mansion was originally built by a navy veteran of the War of 1812, who named the house after his commanding officer, Commodore Oliver Perry. Commodore Perry was famous for saying, "We have met the British, and they are ours." There is a morning room, a well-stocked library, a conservatory, and snooker room, all furnished with heirloom pieces and antiques from Sir Bernard's personal collection, making it look and feel like an English manor house. The library has a secret passageway—a hinged bookshelf that leads into the Morning Room.

The Inn at Perry Cabin has forty-one guest rooms, all exquisitely decorated with lush fabrics and canopy beds. The rooms are luxurious and comfortable; fresh flowers decorate your room, a fireplace is there to keep you cozy. These and other exquisite appointments vie with the views of the Chesapeake Bay.

The Inn is set on twenty-five acres overlooking the Miles River, which feeds into the Bay. Terraces look out onto the meticulously maintained gardens and grounds. The cathedral ceilinged non-smoking restaurant is overseen by Chef Mark Salter. Venetian chandeliers and banks of mullioned windows give this room a romantic aura. And let's not forget the fireplace and candlelight. The restaurant offers an exciting menu featuring local seafood specialties, one of the finest dining experiences in the region. And in keeping with English country-house fashion, afternoon tea is served with scones and clotted cream.

The lawn rolls down to the water, dock, and estuary where the Inn keeps its boats. You can go fishing, sailing, and for cruises on the Chesapeake. There is a golf course nearby. And you can always buzz into St. Michaels to shop for arts, crafts, and antiques. How about a romantic carriage ride through the village? Or a candlelight dinner on the dock? If you want to get the big picture, charter a helicopter ride over the bay. And there's a sunset cruise where you can enjoy cocktails as the sun goes down on another perfect day.

Rates: Rooms $195–$375; Suites $525–$575

THE INN AT PERRY CABIN
308 Watkins Lane
St. Michaels, MD 21663

Phone	(410) 745-2200
Toll free	(800) 722-2949
Fax	(410) 745-3348

Massachusetts

RITZ-CARLTON
Boston

> A single flow'r he sent me, since we met.
>   All tenderly his messenger he chose;
> Deep-hearted, pure, with scented dew still wet—
>   One perfect rose.
>
>   — "One Perfect Rose" by Dorothy Parker

The Ritz is a perfect rose—simple, elegant, immaculate, timeless, and unique. It is also one of the finest hotels in the country, in one of the most romantic cities as well.

An imposing structure serving as the cornerstone of Boston's famous Back Bay, the Ritz, a historic landmark, has a history almost as storied as the city it inhabits. It's a wonder that the hotel was built in 1927 and is still younger than some of its regular patrons. Because Boston used to try out many Broadway plays and musicals, The Ritz has a long history of theatrical inspiration. Richard Rodgers wrote "Ten Cents a Dance" on a piano in his Ritz suite. Tennessee Williams revised *Streetcar Named Desire* here. Oscar Hammerstein wrote the lyrics to "Edelweiss" during one of his stays. Among the celebrities who have stayed at the Ritz are: Winston Churchill, Bob Hope, Frank Sinatra, Cole Porter, Ella Fitzgerald, Charlton Heston, Elton John, Katherine Hepburn, Elizabeth Taylor, Prince Charles, John Wayne…and this is only a partial list.

The Dining Room is one of the best restaurants in town, exquisite offerings in an elegant setting with impeccable service. High tea at the Ritz is a tradition in itself. Share The Lounge, a beautiful tea room with the proper Bostonians and enjoy the colorful, flower-decked view of the Public Gardens and the Swan Pond. But tea is not the only ritual that the Ritz keeps up. Every Valentine's Day the hotel hosts an evening of sinful desserts and intimate dancing. Enjoy a glass of champagne and chocolate fettucini with vanilla anglaise, chocolate crepe suzette, chocolate concorde, chocolate fondue, or white chocolate cappuccino torte in the chocolate buffet. As part of the Valentine's celebration, the flower shop invites children to play cupid and remember mom with a single red rose, priced at just a quarter. Dad can place his own floral order, if one rose isn't enough.

Boston has a charm that is impossible to imitate. A mix of Yankee tradition and urban novelty, Boston has all the amenities of a major city, and yet it still retains the intimate feel of a college town. Have a drink at the Bull and Finch, the bar that *Cheers* was based on. Stroll the cobblestone streets of nearby Beacon Hill, or walk the Freedom Trail. Visit the North End and sample some of the best Italian food this side of Naples. Take a turn on the Esplanade and watch the college crews skull on the Charles River. Head across the water to Harvard Square and tour the ivy-covered campus or catch a concert at Symphony Hall.

Boston is an exciting, historic city, and the Ritz sits in the middle of it all—unspoiled, unwilted, fresh as the day it first bloomed.

Rates: Rooms $245–$385; Suites $325–$1,495

RITZ-CARLTON
15 Arlington Street
Boston, MA 02117

Phone   (617) 536-5700
Toll free   (800) 241-3333
Fax   (617) 496-5020

THE BLANTYRE
Lenox

> It was this moment of love, this fleeting victory over themselves, which had kept them from atrophy and extinction.
>
> —*The House of Mirth* by Edith Wharton

Wharton lived in a "cottage" in Lenox, where she observed the customs and manners of the Eastern upper class as material for her stunning literary creations. And there is still a sense of Gilded Age luxury and serenity to the region.

Yankee cosmopolites still come here every summer to escape the city heat and enjoy the cooler climate of the leafy mountains. Over the years the Berkshires have become a summer resort area with an enviable array of cultural (as well as natural) offerings. And The Blantyre, a Tudor mansion situated on eighty-five acres of meticulously maintained grounds, epitomizes the region's blend of tradition, elegance, and natural beauty.

The Blantyre is a 1905 replica of a Scottish castle. The main house contains twenty-four guest quarters, while the recently renovated Carriage House and several cottages round out the compound. In the main house, the Great Hall has wood paneling, fresh flowers, and antique furnishings.

In keeping with the region's harmonious blend of rural sophistication, The Blantyre offers a wide range of activities, but doesn't make you feel as if you must be doing something. On the grounds there is a swimming pool, four tennis courts, and two croquet lawns. Croquet was a favorite game among the nineteenth-century socialites who first put the Berkshires on the map.

The atmosphere is aristocratic yet comfortable. Rather than having to claim its prestige with fancy trappings, The Blantyre expresses itself with understated elegance. Return guests and travel writers who appreciate this classy ambiance have made The Blantyre one of the most renowned estate inns in the country. Fine French food is served in the formal dining room, where the service is excellent, yet you hardly ever know that it's there. Breakfast is offered in the sun-filled conservatory. And you can also relax in the music salon.

Of course there is life beyond the compound. You can visit Edith Wharton's "cottage," which often provides live readings and other performances. Go to Tanglewood for a concert out on the lawn or in the newly-built performance barn. There's nothing like camping out under the

stars on a blanket, with a jug of wine, a loaf of bread, and
the person you'd most like to be with, listening to the
gorgeous music waft from the concert stage and into the
green mountains beyond. The Boston Symphony plays
here in the summer, and the stage is host to a wide
variety of classical and popular performers. And don't forget the Boston Pops, who are also regulars. There's also
summer theater, ballet, and a host of other attractions.
The Norman Rockwell Museum is nearby.

Rates: Rooms and cottages $175–$485; Suites $300–$625
(Closed from November to April)

THE BLANTYRE
16 Blantyre Road
Lenox, MA 01240

Phone   (413) 637-3556
Fax   (413) 637-4282

■■■■

THE INN AT FERNBROOK AT CAPE COD
Centerville

> Oh, when I was in love with you,
>   Then I was clean and brave,
> And miles around the wander grew
>   How well I did behave.
>
> — "Oh, When I Was in Love" by A.E. Housman

Cape Cod is gorgeous, a narrow spit of land extending
out into the sea, lined with sandy beaches and charming
little towns. But like many gorgeous places, it can also get
pretty crowded. That's why it helps to find a place like
The Inn at Fernbrook.

The Inn was built by Howard Marston, the owner of
the famous Parker House in Boston. Marston had the
estate landscaped by Frederick Law Olmsted, who also
did the landscaping for New York's Central Park, Boston's
Public Gardens, and Golden Gate Park in San Francisco.
Olmsted designed the heart-shaped rose garden that still
adorns the side yard of the estate today.

Purchased by Dr. Herbert Kalmus, the inventor of

technicolor, in the 1930s, Fernbrook became a hot spot for Hollywood celebrities. Then it was deeded to the Archidiocese of New York and converted into a summer retreat for Cardinal Spellman. In 1986, Brian Gallo and Sal DiFlorio bought Fernbrook and restored it to its original elegance.

The Inn at Fernbrook has acres of grounds for intimate wandering. Take a relaxing stroll along the grounds, each square foot meticulously landscaped and maintained. The lake is decorated with water lilies. Fish ponds, rock gardens, and a cool, quiet arbor create a sense of pastoral splendor.

There are seven guest accommodations at the Inn. Recommended is Cardinal Spellman's former chapel, furnished with a canopied bed, fireplace, and stained glass window. If you want complete privacy, ask for the Garden Cottage, a separate house with its own white picket fence.

You might find The Inn at Fernbrook so romantic you want to get married there; in fact, many couples do. The Inn's rose garden makes a great setting for weddings, and you can book the whole Inn for your wedding party.

Rates: Rooms $125–$185

THE INN AT FERNBROOK AT CAPE COD
481 Main Street
Centerville, MA 02632

Phone   (508) 775-4334
Fax   (508) 778-4455

▬▬

THORNCROFT INN
Vineyard Haven

> Don't hurry with their tender dew,
> Sweetness complete and incomplete;
> For I have lived to wait for you:
> My heart was your approaching feet.
>
> — "The Footsteps" by Paul Valéry

If you want to go further out along the Cape, try Martha's

Vineyard. Again, the crowds in summertime can be a bit pressing, but Thorncroft Inn gives you a peaceful setting that offers both convenient location and picturesque privacy. Set on three-and-a-half acres (a lot of property on Martha's Vineyard), the Thorncroft Inn features fourteen guest rooms. Eight of the rooms are in the main house, while five others are in the carriage house, these are the largest suites on the property. There is also a one-bedroom deluxe cottage available. Ten of the rooms have fireplaces. Some of them have jacuzzis. All the bedrooms include two bathrobes, turndown service, morning paper, and a full country breakfast in bed.

The dining room has a fireplace and decorative wall coverings. The Inn has a state-of-the art telecommunications system, so you can keep in touch with the office, if you must. But you shouldn't. There's too much else to do here on the Vineyard. The Inn is just a short walk from the docks of Vineyard Haven. You can walk along the beach or just lay back on the sand. Shopping and rubbernecking for celebrities are among the other offerings of this exclusive island community.

"We greet all our guests personally," says owner Lynn Buder, who runs the Inn with her husband, Karl. "We sit down with them when they arrive. This gives them a chance to meet us and gives us a chance to get a feel for them. Some want to just relax. Some want to only sightsee. Some want to do nothing at all."

And Martha's Vineyard is a fine place for doing just that.

Rates: Rooms $200–$275; Suites $350–$425;
       Cottages $250–$500 (based upon season)

THORNCROFT INN
460 Main Street
Vineyard Haven, MA 02568

Phone	(508) 693-3333
Toll free	(800) 332-1236
Fax	(508) 693-5419

Michigan

THE GRAND HOTEL
Mackinac Island

> Tis not how witty nor how free,
> Nor yet how beautiful she be,
> But how much kind and true to me.
> Freedom and wit none can confine
> And beauty like the sun doth shine,
> But kind and true are only mine.
>
> — "Kind and True" by Aurelian Townshend

A stately presence on secluded Mackinac Island, The Grand Hotel is a great place for a Midwestern getaway. The Indians called this island Michilimackinac, or the Great Turtle, because that's what it looks like from the mainland. And like turtles, visitors to Mackinac Island like to hide away and escape into privacy.

Originally built in 1887, The Grand retains its historic charm. Situated on a high bluff overlooking the straits of Mackinac, the hotel commands a breathtaking view. No cars are allowed on Mackinac Island, so when you step off the ferry a horse-drawn carriage will take you to the hotel. Once you arrive, footmen in white gloves will greet you and take you inside to the Victorian decorated lobby.

Or you might want to linger on the "world's largest porch," a comfortable Victorian affair replete with wicker furniture, a picturesque spot for relaxing conversation and people-watching. Or you could take a turn on the expansive and meticulously gardened grounds. Eventually, you'll want to see your room, one of the hotel's 325 individually decorated guest accommodations. Among the most unique lodgings is the Wicker Suite, furnished with a brass bed and white wicker furniture.

Dining at The Grand is an experience to savor. The food is exquisite, and the atmosphere is unbeatable. At the main dining room local, fresh-caught seafood is a specialty, and many dishes are garnished with Michigan cherries. Jackets and ties are required at dinner, which is a five-course affair. After dinner, relax over coffee in the Parlour or enjoy cocktails at the Geranium and Wine Bars. The Grand Stand offers lighter fare, and the pool grill provides snacks and beverages. Afternoon tea is served in the lobby, accompanied by a string quartet.

Live music and ballroom dancing are specialties here at The Grand. Dinner is accompanied by an orchestra, and there is a small dance floor in the dining room. After dinner, the dancing continues in the Terrace Room, where The Grand Hotel Dance Band plays in the manner of the great bands of the 1930s and 1940s.

When you're not cutting a rug, there are other activities to enjoy. The hotel has a huge swimming pool and acres of grounds to walk through. There's a private golf course for duffers. Tennis courts and nature trails offer a pleasant workout. You can rent bicycles or saddle horses to get around the island. Take a scenic tour of this beautiful and historic island in a vis-à-vis, an antique carriage drawn by horses in dress harness.

Rates: Rooms $290–$440; Suites $550

THE GRAND HOTEL
Mackinac Island, MI 49757

Phone   (906) 847-3331
Toll free   (800) 334-7263
Fax   (906) 847-3259

THE TOWNSEND HOTEL
Birmingham

Love is its own great loveliness alway,
And takes new lustre from the touch of time;
Its bough owns no December and no May,
But bears its blossom into Winter's clime.

— "Love" by Thomas Hood

Whether you're in Detroit on business or spending a weekend visiting this city's attractions, The Townsend Hotel is a charming, classy place to stay. Located in Birmingham, one of the Motor City's most elite suburbs, it's a comfortable thirty minutes from downtown Detroit—away from the city grit, noise, and hassles. Yet the Townsend is also convenient to many of the delights of this surprising city.

A European-style, intimate hotel, which focuses on personalized service, The Townsend has eighty-seven rooms. Entering the lobby, you'll be impressed by the cherry paneling and marble floors. An eighteenth-century English mantelpiece hangs over the marble fireplace, and light sparkles down from the Waterford chandelier. Afternoon tea is served here in the style of the great British manor homes, with pastries from the hotel's own bakery and tea served on Royal Doulton china.

Rooms are decorated in period furnishings and traditional decor, with dark woods, damask upholstery, and cotton chintz. Forty-eight suites have private balconies. Three exclusive corner suites provide separate living and dining areas, and butler pantries. The Rugby Grille features excellent American and continental fare served by candlelight. It's also a popular spot with the locals for power breakfasts and lunch buffets.

Service at The Townsend is exquisite, personalized, and professional. Everyone from the doorman to the switchboard operator greets you by name. The maid leaves you a treat at nightly turndown. And the concierge staff is there to meet your every need. Truly a splendid experience, whether you venture out of your hotel room or simply spend all your time in elegant privacy.

Rates: Rooms $225; Suites $260–$475

THE TOWNSEND HOTEL
100 Townsend Street
Birmingham, MI 48009

Phone	(810) 642-7900
Toll free	(800) 548-4172
Fax	(810) 645-9061

Minnesota

THE WHITNEY HOTEL
Minneapolis

> Rose leaves, when the rose is dead,
> Are heaped for the beloved's bed;
> And so thy thoughts, when thou art gone,
> Love itself shall slumber on.
>
> — "Music" by Percy Bysshe Shelley

The European elegance that was once a characteristic aspect of the Mississippi riverfront is back on display in The Whitney Hotel. This lavish and classy establishment, which many say is the only place to stay in Minneapolis/ St. Paul, serves two distinct clientele. During the week, this is a downtown hotel for people visiting the Twin Cities on business. But on the weekend it becomes a romantic retreat for Minnesotans and out-of-towners looking for love in a cold climate.

Overlooking St. Anthony Falls, The Whitney offers a quiet elegance in an nineteenth-century European motif. Special Weekend package offerings start with a bilevel suite, champagne, and breakfast for two in The Whitney Grille for only $190. But the ultimate Whitney experience is the Romantic Weekend. Book the luxurious Penthouse Suite, and the hotel will give you a private cocktail party with a pianist to entertain you. The Penthouse Suite has a whirlpool bath, a baby grand piano, fireplace, and a balcony with a spectacular view. After you are welcomed to your suite you can lounge on the patio overlooking the Falls, or use your personal Lincoln Town Car to tour the Twin Cities. At the end of a busy day, you can unwind in the jacuzzi before your private cocktail party and dinner. After dinner, a late night snack of fruits, cheese, and desserts await you in your suite. Breakfast the next morning can be enjoyed either in the restaurant or in the privacy of your suite.

The Whitney Grille is one of the top restaurants in Minneapolis, featuring classic American cuisine in an intimate setting amid a warm, wood-paneled decor. The dining room is quiet and intimate, perfect for a cozy dinner for two. A flower-decked garden plaza offers a pleasant setting for summer repasts.

The hotel is conveniently located in downtown Minneapolis on the riverfront area. From there it's easy to get to the Hennepin Center for the Arts, Orchestra Hall, the Metrodome, and other Twin Cities' attractions.

Rates: Rooms $155–$200; Suites $200–$300

THE WHITNEY HOTEL
150 Portland Avenue
Minneapolis, MN 55401

Phone	(612) 339-9300
Toll free	(800) 248-1879
Fax	(612) 339-1333

Mississippi

CEDAR GROVE MANSION
Vicksburg

> My mistress, when she walks, treads on the ground:
> And yet, by heaven, I think my love as rare
> As any she belied with false compare.
>
> — "Sonnet 130" by William Shakespeare

Mississippi is a place of moonlight and magnolias, the romantic past remembered and restored. Life here is unhurried, and attention is paid to the simpler pleasures. You don't have to be a native to enjoy Mississippi's stately elegance or rich history. The famous southern hospitality here at Cedar Grove will quickly make you feel like a native southerner, or at least dispel any lingering impression that you're just another carpetbagger.

Originally built by John Klein as a wedding present for his wife, Cedar Grove was finished less than a decade before the Civil War. The battle of Vicksburg was a turning point in the war between the states when, after a brutal forty-seven day siege, the town finally fell to Union forces under General Ulysses S. Grant. Luckily, Cedar Grove survived the onslaught, although a Union cannonball still remains lodged in the parlor wall. Mrs. Klein, a niece of Union General William Tecumseh Sherman, left the cannonball there to prove that she received no special consideration from her uncle or his troops. Today Cedar Grove has been faithfully preserved and improved and stands as one of the South's largest and most beautiful historic mansions.

Cedar Grove has an unparalleled collection of antebellum furniture, giving it a true sense of history and tradition. Gaslight chandeliers flicker against gold-leaf mirrors. The mantelpieces are made of Italian marble that the Kleins fell in love with on their European honey-

97

moon. Situated on a four-acre estate, Cedar Grove boasts sculpted gardens, gazebos, and running fountains. Jefferson Davis once danced in the ornate ballroom. The beautiful and stately library is a perfect setting for after-dinner conversation. Truly this is authentic southern elegance, the kind that cannot be imitated or faked.

Three separate residences are available. The guest house has two bedrooms and a swimming pool set into a brick courtyard. The Carriage House contains eight suites. Make sure and ask for one with a fireplace. The master bedroom, the most well-appointed room in the main house, is named after General Grant, not a terribly popular character in these parts.

Once you come to Cedar Grove, you might not want to leave. The atmosphere is one of historic charm and southern warmth, and you'll feel as if you are personal guests of the owners. But don't miss the opportunity to tour scenic Vicksburg and the mighty Mississippi River, Father of the Waters.

Rates: Suites $85–$165; Guest Houses $120–$135

CEDAR GROVE MANSION
2200 Oak Street
Vicksburg, MS 39180

Phone	(601) 636-1605
Toll free	(800) 862-1300
Fax	(601) 634-6126

▬▬▬

Missouri

THE CROWNE PLAZA MAJESTIC HOTEL
St. Louis

> And the eyes forget the tears they have shed,
> The heart forgets its sorrow and ache;
> The soul partakes the season's youth,
> And the sulfurous rifts of passion and woe
> Lie deep ëneath a silence pure and smooth,
> Like burnt-out craters healed with snow.
>
> — "What Is So Rare As a Day in June?"
> by James Russell Lowell

The Crowne Plaza Majestic is a beautifully restored, historic hotel right in downtown St. Louis. Originally opened in 1914, the building is constructed in Renaissance Revival style and has been placed on the national list of Historic Places. While the original building had 240 rooms, the renovation has reduced that to ninety-one, so the guest quarters are now much larger and more comfortable. There are only three suites, but the king- and queen-sized doubles are spacious and well-appointed. The rooms are furnished in Old World style with all the modern amenities, all individually decorated with chaise lounges, marble vanities, and poster beds.

Guests are treated like royalty during their stay at The Crowne Plaza Majestic; the hotel offers their guests turndown service with chocolates, in-room coffee served on a silver tray, and a host of complimentary services. A concierge service tends to the needs of guests with prompt yet unobtrusive service. That and other individualized services is why they call the hotel "a private residence for people away from home."

While The Crowne Plaza Majestic once had one of the best restaurants in the Midwest, Chef Rick Johns has departed, and the jury is still out on his replacement. But

The Crowne Plaza Majestic still has Just Jazz, one of the top jazz spots in the country. Sit and sip a cocktail while listening to the dulcet tones of a blues singer or to the silver-throated song of a saxophone.

The Crowne Plaza Majestic offers unbeatable downtown convenience. It is just blocks away from Busch Stadium. Nearby is Kiel auditorium. Only a short walk away is the Gateway Arch and waterfront parks. Or you can take a ride on one of the Mississippi riverboats docked at Laclede's landing.

Rates: Rooms $155–$175; Suites $250–$550

THE CROWNE PLAZA MAJESTIC HOTEL
1019 Pine Street
St. Louis, MO 63101

Phone	(314) 436-2355
Toll free	(800) 451-2355
Fax	(314) 436-0223

Montana

TRIPLE CREEK RANCH
Darby

> I would not fear the muscling-in of love
> If I were tickled by the urchin hunger
> Rehearsing heat upon a raw-edged nerve.
> I would not fear the devil in the loin
> Nor the outspoken grave.
>
> — "If I Were Tickled by the Rub of Love"
>   by Dylan Thomas

This romantic mountain hideaway in the Big Sky state combines rugged beauty and plush elegance. Adjacent to millions of acres of scenic Rocky Mountain wilderness near the Idaho border, you can't get much more secluded than Triple Creek. But seclusion doesn't mean you have to skimp on creature comforts. This resort has all the amenities you could wish for. And it's couples only, so you're ensured the quiet and privacy you seek for a romantic escape.

Triple Creek is located at the foot of Trapper Peak just outside Darby, a small town a little more than an hour south of Missoula. The ranch features eighteen cabins of which three accommodate two couples with two baths. These cabins all have spectacular views of the creek and nearby mountains. Each cabin has a fireplace, fully stocked refrigerator, and wet bar. The large cabin suites feature separate living rooms, huge baths, and private hot tubs on the scenic decks. A perfect place to tickle the rub of love.

The main lodge has a cozy bar with a wood-burning fireplace and an excellent dining room, which serves complimentary wine with its gourmet cuisine. The dining room's executive chef, Chef Martha McGinnis, has been featured in *Southern Living* and *The Hideaway Reports*.

After dinner you can groove to live music in the bar or sip a postprandial potation in the hot tub. There's one staff member for every guest, so you are assured personalized and efficient service.

Sporting activities are wide and varied. You can swim in the outdoor pool or play tennis. Fly fish in the stream that runs through the resort. Or watch the herd of buffalo kept by the ranch. Nearby is the Bitterroot River, made famous by the book and movie *A River Runs Through It*. Further along is the equally famous Salmon River, great for rafting trips down the dramatic rapids. Horseback riding is also available. Or you can explore the many hiking trails. In the winter enjoy cross-country skiing, snowmobiling, and sleigh rides. Downhill ski areas are only a half hour away.

Like most of the region, Triple Creek is laid back and unpretentious, a perfect romantic getaway for those who want to enjoy the wild country in comfort and pleasure.

Rates: Cabins $475–$995

TRIPLE CREEK RANCH
5551 West Fork Stage Route K
Darby, MT 59829

Phone	(406) 821-4600
Toll free	(800) 654-2943
Fax	(406) 821-4666

Nevada

THE MIRAGE HOTEL AND CASINO
Las Vegas

> Cupid from his favourite nation
> Care and envy will remove;
> Jealousy, that poisons passion,
> And despair, that dies for love.

> — "Fairest Isle" by John Dryden

Cupid can strike just about anywhere, and he has terrific accuracy in Las Vegas. Some people find Vegas terribly romantic; just about everyone calls it exciting; and absolutely everyone thinks it's fascinating. Where else in the world can you get prime rib for $3 served to you by an out-of-work Elvis impersonator? Whether you're a big-time player or just in town for a convention, there's no reason not to have a little romance in this twenty-four-hour city. Who knows, you might even wind up getting married at one of the many wedding chapels. Or if you're already hitched, you could rediscover some of that spark you might have lost at home. Vegas is a place where absolutely anything can happen, and usually does.

The place to stay in Vegas is the spectacular Mirage. Located right on the strip, The Mirage is hard to miss. It's the one with the huge man-made volcano that erupts every night, belching flames hundreds of feet into the air and illuminating the five-story high waterfalls that tumble down through the lush tropical foliage into the glimmering lagoon pools. This is the prime attraction on the strip, drawing huge crowds every night.

But the spectacle doesn't stop there. Once in the lobby of The Mirage you'll see the 20,000-gallon aquarium, which runs the length of the check-in desk. The aquarium is filled with more than a thousand different fish and other specimens, including several sharks. The lobby also has a ninety-foot-high atrium with several exotic species of tropical plants.

The Mirage is a world unto itself, offering everything you could ever possibly want, and then some. It has three towers of rooms on some one hundred acres of prime real estate. One of the several swimming areas is a huge Polynesian-style pool, with several cabanas for liquid refreshment. Nearby is the dolphin habitat, where five dolphins cavort in a 1.5 million gallon pool. Vegas' world famous magician team Siegfried and Roy perform exclusively at The Mirage. The Mirage also has a men's and women's spa and an on-site gym, with a personal trainer available to pump you up. The hotel's salon offers herbal and seaweed wraps, as well as facials and hairstyling.

The Mirage has a vast array of restaurants, ranging from traditional Kokomo's, to the Japanese Mikado, to Chinese fare at the Moongate. Ristorante Riva features Northern Italian cuisine, while the Bistro serves French food on its own cobblestone street.

Oh, and there's also a casino at The Mirage, offering all the tables, slots, and games you could ask for.

Rates: Rooms $79–$349; Suites $375–$1,000

THE MIRAGE HOTEL AND CASINO
3400 Las Vegas Boulevard
Las Vegas, NV 89109

Phone	(702) 791-7111
Toll free	(800) 627-6667
Fax	(702) 791-7414

▰▰▰▰

New Mexico

DOS CASAS VIEJAS
Santa Fe

> Light, so low in the vale
> > You flash and lighten afar,
> For this is the golden morning of love,
> > And you are his morning star.

> — "Marriage Morning" by Alfred, Lord Tennyson

Dos Casas Viejas on Agua Fria Street, Spanish for two old houses on cold water street. Dos Casas is not so much a hotel as a little village, a pair of houses built in the 1860s with eighteen-inch thick adobe walls set on a half-acre private compound. The houses are constructed in wonderful, soothing architecture. And the ambiance is comfortable and homey. It's conveniently located—only a ten-minute walk from the Plaza, a famous shopping district.

Dos Casas is geared toward providing peace and quiet. The bed-and-breakfast-style lodging specializes in honeymoons and anniversary celebrations. A professional and discreet staff knows how to cater to a couple's needs without being intrusive. The five guest quarters each have their own private entrance and walled patio for the ultimate in serene seclusion. Geraniums, pansies, petunias, and clematises bloom on the patios. Wood-burning fireplaces warm each room.

Morning is a special time at Dos Casas, whether it's your marriage morning or just another day in paradise together. You can eat breakfast pool side or have it brought to your room to enjoy without getting out of bed. Later on in the day, enjoy a pleasant repast in the dining area, furnished with hickory wood tables and cowhide chairs. After dinner relax in the sitting room and

library and share a few laughs with the other guests of
Dos Casa Viejas.

Rates: Rooms $165–$175; Suites $225–$275

DOS CASAS VIEJAS
610 Agua Fria Street
Santa Fe, NM 87501

Phone   (505) 983-1636
Fax   (505) 983-1749

▬▬▬▬

INN OF THE ANASAZI
Santa Fe

> We made love on a winter afternoon
> and when we woke, hours had turned and changed,
> the moon was shining, and the earth was new.
>   — "Winter Poem" by Frederick Morgan

They call New Mexico the Land of Enchantment, and it's
easy to see why. There's something almost mystical about
the desert mountains, the spectacular sunsets, the Native
American heritage and southwestern culture. Here is a
place where time seems to stand still, and every day the
ancient earth is renewed once again.

Of course, Santa Fe is the most exciting and romantic
city in New Mexico. And the Inn of the Anasazi is the
place to stay here. Located right in the heart of Santa Fe,
near the galleries and shops of the historic main plaza,
the Inn is a luxurious, yet intimate, resort, converted into
a Pueblo-style hotel from its original incarnation as a
glass municipal building.

The Inn is named after the Anasazi Indians, who were
the earliest inhabitants of this region, so entrenched that
the Navajos called them "the ancient ones." They built
dwellings in cliffsides, such as Mesa Verde and Chaco
Canyon, and established highly developed farming
communities. Their legacy is continued at the Inn, which
recaptures the patterned masonry techniques and colorful
murals favored by the Anasazi. The common rooms have
smooth-plastered walls and ceilings with rough-hewn

wood vigas and latillas, traditional support beams. The wrought-iron lighting fixtures and snake-patterned sconces provide a romantic glow downstairs. The upstairs is lit with rope-patterned floor lamps and more traditional ironwork fixtures. Kava fireplaces warm the library and boardroom. The wine cellar has painted, hand-carved wooden doors.

The Inn features fifty-nine guest rooms and eight deluxe rooms. All the rooms are furnished with four poster beds, entertainment centers, and gas-burning fireplaces. The suites have fax machines and stereos, for those who don't want to completely cut themselves off from civilization. Hand-crafted rugs and Anasazi-styled bedding give the rooms a distinctive southwestern feel. The bathrooms are decorated in handmade Mexican tile.

The famous Anasazi Restaurant combines Native American, New Mexican, and cowboy cuisine into a fascinating and tantalizing dining experience. After dinner, relax by the fireside in the living room or browse the legends of the Southwest in the cultural library.

Convenient to every attraction in Santa Fe, the Inn is a perfect jumping off point for tours of the Southwest. You can visit the ancient Indian ruins and sites of the Anasazi and Pueblo. Fishing, hiking, rafting, and skiing tours can be arranged by the Inn's staff.

The Inn of the Anasazi is consistently ranked the best lodging in Santa Fe by a wide range of travel experts.

Rates: Rooms $199–$345; Deluxe Rooms $345–$395
    (based upon season)

INN OF THE ANASAZI
113 Washington Avenue
Santa Fe, NM 87501

Phone	(505) 988-3030
Toll free	(800) 688-8100
Fax	(505) 988-3277

New York

OLD DROVERS INN
Dover Plains

> My heart is like a singing bird
>   Whose nest is in a watered shoot;
> My heart is like an apple-tree
>   Whose boughs are bent with thick-set fruit;
> My heart is like a rainbow shell
>   That paddles in a halcyon sea;
> My heart is gladder than all these,
>   Because my love is come to me.
>
> — "A Birthday" by Christina Rossetti

Nearby the scenic Hudson River and at the entry to the Berkshire Moutains, Dover Plains and the surrounding area of Dutchess and Columbia counties offer rustic charm and natural beauty without sacrificing the pleasures of civilization. Only ninety minutes north of New York City, you'll feel as if you are in a completely different world. And you are. This is the old New York of Dutch Patrons and stagecoaches running from Albany to Manhattan. Rolling hills dotted with farm pastures and acres of spectacular foliage, this is one of the most beautiful places in the Northeast.

Operated continuously since 1750 (which doesn't even qualify it for the oldest inn in the county, a claim that goes to Rhinebeck's Beekman Arms) the Old Drovers Inn is an atmospheric country retreat in the Colonial style. Downstairs is the cozy library, filled with both classics and bestsellers. Upstairs are the four guest rooms. Three of the rooms have fireplaces, so make sure you get one of them. The best accommodation is the Meeting Room, which offers a high ceiling, fireplace, and two antique double beds. Antique furnishings and luxurious amenities adorn every room. The house is a bit creaky, as one would expect from a building that old. But that's precisely its charm. And it has been marvelously restored.

The restaurant, Tap Room, where Chef Jeffrey Marquise creates such marvels as Lobster Hash with B&B Corn Sauce, is justly renowned. The elegant, low-beamed tap room with huge fireplace is comfortably rustic. It's closed on Tuesdays and Wednesdays (except in October), which gives you a chance to visit some of the many other excellent dining establishments nearby, including the Culinary Institute of America, where you can sample what the finest chef's school in America is cooking up.

The owners of the Old Drovers Inn used to visit the place themselves. They fell in love with it and wound up purchasing the property on Valentine's Day. It's a romantic place run by true romantics. And there's always a special Valentine's Day celebration at the Inn.

The best time of year to visit is fall, where you can enjoy the scenic splendors of an upstate autumn. Watch the leaves turn color, and pick some apples from one of the many orchards nearby. Go for a drive up scenic Route 22 or along the Hudson River. Tour the historic mansions along the Hudson River, or go antique shopping in the many charming villages nearby.

Rates: Rooms $150–$395
        (Closed the first three weeks of January)

OLD DROVERS INN
Route 22
Box 675
Dover Plains, NY 12522

Phone   (914) 832-9311
Fax   (914) 832-6356

New York City has the most of everything, and it certainly isn't lacking in romance. That's why we've included four hotels in the Big Apple, so that you can find that special place, whether you're a first time visitor or you consider it your second home.

THE BOX TREE HOTEL
New York City

> Who shall hear of us
> in the time to come?
> Let him say there was
> a burst of fragrance
> from black branches.

> — "Love Song" by William Carlos Williams

Unique, even idiosyncratic, The Box Tree Hotel is a very special place, perfect for romantic visitors who seek to avoid the ordinary and embark upon an adventure that is guaran-teed to please. Situated right in Midtown Manhattan, among the glass and steel skyscrapers of Third Avenue, this hotel sits on a quiet, tree-lined block of townhouses. The location is unbeatable, you are right around the corner from Lutece, one of New York's finest restaurants. The United Nations is nearby. And the Broadway theater district, where scores of spectacular musicals and gripping dramas are restating New York's preeminence as the theater capital of the world, is a quick cab ride across town.

Entering The Box Tree you walk into an intimate reception area with a polished brick floor. A custom fireplace is framed by eighteenth-century Italian porcelain figures supporting the mantel. Messages are dis-cretely left for guests in the antique Spanish campaign chest next to a Louis XIII chair. An art noveau staircase leads up to the guest quarters. There is no elevator in the building, so you will spend a bit of time huffing up and down the elegant stairways.

Twelve mini-suites are equally divided between the main townhouse and one adjoining. The rooms are not large, but they are exquisitely and individually designed.

One has a Chinese motif, another Egyptian, another Japanese. All rooms have fireplaces, with settees or sofas facing them. Turndown service includes a chestnut-glace, instead of the standard hotel chocolate or mint.

The restaurant at The Box Tree is ornately designed in baroque and Tiffany styling. And the menu is equally extravagant. Entrées may include such delicacies as broiled salmon sauce mousseline or sweetbreads with truffles and madeira. Desserts are a specialty here, like vacherin "Box Tree," poached pears in beaujolais, crème brûlée, and cocotte of raspberries.

Come see why some people call this "the best little boudoir in New York City."

Rates: Suites $190–$330 ($100 credit towards dinner is applied)

THE BOX TREE HOTEL
250 East 49th Street
New York, NY 10017

Phone   (212) 758-8320
Fax   (212) 308-3899

THE CARLYLE
New York City

> Wild nights! Wild nights!
> Were I with thee,
> Wild nights should be
> Our luxury!
>
> — "Out of the Morning" by Emily Dickinson

The Carlyle is luxury itself. This justly famous hotel is resplendent with charm and sophistication, a city unto itself. Located in Manhattan's Upper East Side, The Carlyle is convenient to museums, shops, and theaters, yet away from the Midtown bustle. There are plenty of fantastic art galleries and specialty stores on Madison Avenue alone, but with all New York has to offer, there's no reason to stay close to home. At the very least, visit nearby Central Park for a romantic walk or carriage ride.

Step into the lobby at The Carlyle, and you know you're in a first-class establishment. The black and white marble vestibule leads to a serene open space exquisitely decorated with Aubusson carpets and Gobelin tapestries. Beyond is the Gallery, done in an exotic Turkish style, a great place for people-watching. The Carlyle has 190 rooms, each one individually decorated and equipped with porcelain lamps and vases, chintz coverlets, antique satin boudoir chairs, mini-bars, hair dryers, VCRs, stereo cassettes, and CD players. The marble bathrooms are all appointed with whirlpool baths. Some even have bidets. Nancy Reagan's favorite, the 1812 Room, has fourteen-foot ceilings and an early nineteenth-century Chinese screen.

The Carlyle Restaurant offers some of the most superbly prepared French classical and contemporary cuisine in a city full of great restaurants. In three dining areas, guests are seated between English hunting prints and French engravings. The menu offers a Dover sole which *W* magazine calls the best in Manhattan. Or try the breast of chicken with morels and a coulis of foie gras. Sunday brunch is famous for paupierre of swordfish with wild mushroom ravioli and croustade of scrambled eggs with salmon and caviar. The wine selection is among the best in the world. And Bemelmans Bar features Barbara Carroll and other entertainers five nights a week.

But perhaps the most famous offering of The Carlyle is the inimitable Bobby Short, who has been performing in the Cafe Carlyle for more than two decades. Other entertainers showcased in the Cafe have been the Modern Jazz Quartet and Dixie Carter.

Rates: Rooms $295–$430; Suites $500–$2,000

THE CARLYLE
35 East 76th Street
New York, NY 10021

Phone	(212) 744-1600
Toll free	(800) 227-5737
Fax	(212) 744-0958

THE LOWELL HOTEL
New York City

> She was a phantom of delight
> When first she gleamed upon my sight;
> A lovely apparition, sent
> To be a moment's ornament;
> Her eyes as stars of twilight fair;
> Like twilight's, too, her dusky hair;
> But all things else about her drawn
> From May-time and the cheerful dawn;
> A dancing shape, an image gay,
> To haunt, to startle, and waylay.
>
> — "She Was a Phantom of Delight"
>   by William Wordsworth

Another intimate, unique hotel with a fantastic location is The Lowell Hotel. Situated on a quiet, tree-lined side street on Manhattan's Upper East Side, The Lowell Hotel is a residential hotel that caters to visitors who seek the convenience of Midtown with the elegance of Manhattan's most exclusive neighborhood. It's just a few blocks away from Fifth Avenue and "museum mile" where you can view the priceless artworks of the Metropolitan Museum or the modern paintings and sculptures of the stunningly designed Guggenheim.

When you arrive at The Lowell Hotel, a liveried doorman greets you, leading you to an Empire style reception desk where there is never a registration line. The lobby decor combines art deco with French Empire for an eccentric yet tasteful ambiance. Just off the lobby is the famous Post House Restaurant, one of the best steak houses in New York. The charming Pembroke Room is a great spot for power breakfasts among New York's elite. Lunch, English high tea, and cocktails are also served in the Pembroke.

Management runs The Lowell like a *pied à terre* for their guests, many of whom are frequent return visitors. Celebrities often stay here, although the hotel is protective of their privacy and does not provide a list of famous guests. However, history records that Scott and Zelda Fitzgerald, and Eugene O'Neill and his wife Carlotta all made The Lowell Hotel their home. And rumor has it that the Rolling Stones make it their New York address. The hotel offers forty-eight suites and thirteen deluxe rooms, all of which are uniquely decorated with antiques and fine furnishings. The suites have original art prints, Chinese porcelain, wood-burning fireplaces, libraries, full kitchens, and marble baths with brass fixtures. Ten suites also have private terraces. The Gym Suite has a private, fully equipped exercise room with a breathtaking view of Manhattan.

A special Weekend package includes a luxurious one-bedroom suite, champagne on arrival, and continental breakfast for two in either the Pembroke Room or in the privacy of your suite.

Rates: Rooms $295–$385; Suites $485–$955

THE LOWELL HOTEL
28 East 63rd Street
New York, NY 10021

Phone	(212) 838-1400
Toll free	(800) 221-4444
Fax	(212) 319-4230

THE MAIDSTONE ARMS
East Hampton

> Wi' lightsome heart I pu'd a rose,
>   Upon its thorny tree
> But my fause luver staw my rose,
>   And left the thorn wi' me.
>
> — "The Banks o Doon" by Robert Burns

Long Island's Hamptons offer a classy escape from New York City. Here you can hob-nob with celebrities or take a quiet walk on the beach. With lots of great restaurants and nightclubs, East Hampton is a lively vacation destination. And its charming village, beautiful houses, and peaceful beaches are perfect for a romantic weekend or summer vacation.

The recently renovated Maidstone Arms is right on

Main Street on the historic village green of East Hampton, near the house where "Home Sweet Home" was written, and convenient to the restaurants, shopping, and other attractions of town. The Maidstone has sixteen guest rooms and two cottages, which are preferred for their private intimacy. The restaurant has two dining rooms, with tables draped in crisp white damask and windows draped in summery yellow and white stripes. Fresh seafood is The Maidstone's specialty, but other dishes are also delectable.

Director Gordon Campbell-Gray is a Scottish aristocrat and celebrates Hogmanay, a traditional Scottish year-end holiday at the Inn. After being served welcoming cocktails and afternoon tea, guests enjoy a five-course dinner of Scottish rarities including haggis (a delicacy of minced lamb, smoked salmon, and beef). At midnight the champagne bottles pop open and everybody sings.

Rates: Rooms $180–$295; Cottages $325
     (based on season)

THE MAIDSTONE ARMS
207 Main Street
East Hampton, NY 11937

Phone	(516) 324-5006
Fax	(516) 324-5037

If you'd prefer more private accommodations in East Hampton, how about renting a luxury villa? The Rounick House, an English Tudor style mansion with 295 feet of ocean frontage is available for rent. The house has an indoor and outdoor pool, billiard room, formal dining room, living room, and library. With seven bedrooms, it can sleep fourteen people. Or you can keep it all to yourselves.

Rates: $200,000 (for the summer)

Contact: Charles Bullock
Allan M. Schneider and Associates

Phone	(516) 324-3900
Fax	(516) 324-3557

THE PLAZA HOTEL
New York City

> Who carved Love
>   and placed him by
> this fountain,
>   thinking
> he could control
>   such fire
> with water?

— "A Statue of Eros" by Zenodotos

For some people, this is the center of the world. Fifth Avenue and Central Park South, the heart of uptown Manhattan, and The Plaza standing in the midst of it all. There's nothing more romantic than a twilight carriage ride from The Plaza's doorway through Central Park. The Plaza has been immortalized in countless movies, including *Breakfast at Tiffany's, North By Northwest,* and *Arthur.* And the hotel's gorgeous fountain, made famous as a swimming pool by F. Scott and Zelda Fitzgerald, and many other reckless imitators, is a scene that sums up romance New York style.

The Plaza is a place that dreams are made of. As Frank Lloyd Wright described the hotel, "It's genuine. I like it almost as much as if I'd built it myself." The building is both a New York City and a National Historic Landmark. Recently taken over by Fairmont Hotels and completely renovated, it has lost none of its historic charm or elegance.

There are a grand total of 805 rooms in The Plaza, ninety-six of which are suites. All rooms have crystal chandeliers, and 450 rooms and suites have marble fireplaces. One of the more luxurious accommodations at The Plaza is the Presidential Suite, with more than 7,000-square-feet overlooking Central Park, two living rooms, a dining room, five and a half bedrooms, a 2,000 bottle wine cellar, butler suite and limousine service. If that's a bit rich for your blood, try one of the many other exquisite suites and rooms.

The Oak Bar is one of the most famous meeting spots in Manhattan. Sit and sip a cocktail while you look out onto Central Park South and the park beyond. Nearby is the Oak Room, serving hearty entrées and featuring piano music nightly. The Edwardian Room remains New York's prime location for power breakfasts and pre-theater dinners. The Palm Court is an enchanting European style cafe featuring traditional tea, caviar menu, light supper, or after-dinner cocktails accompanied by romantic violin and piano music. The Oyster Bar is one of the city's top seafood restaurants.

The Plaza has a state-of-the-art exercise room, and offers its guests use of the exclusive Atrium Health Club and Cardio Fitness Center, both within walking distance. There's a concierge desk in the lobby, and the staff is headed by four concierges who are all members of the prestigious Les Clefs d'Or, an international society of concierges who work exclusively in hotel lobbies, which excludes concierges in commercial buildings. The on-premises shops are a classy mall in themselves, including an art gallery, chocolate shop, florist, jewelers, and men's and lady's furnishings. The Cinema 3 features first-run movies. And of course, you're right in the heart of New York City, convenient to Broadway theaters, midtown and uptown restaurants, and everything else this great city has to offer.

Rates: Rooms $290–$550; Suites $425–$15,000
        (based upon season)

THE PLAZA HOTEL
Fifth Avenue at Central Park South
New York, NY 10019

Phone	(212) 759-3000
Toll free	(800) 759-3000
Fax	(212) 759-3167

THE POINT
Saranac Lake

> She let herself be loved: then drowsy-eyed,
> Smiled down from her high couch in languid ease.
> My love was deep and gentle as the seas
> And rose to her as to a cliff the tide.

> — "The Jewels" by Charles Baudelaire

If you enjoy high-class service in rustic solitude, this is the place for you. Deep in the Adirondack Forest, this former Rockefeller family compound is located on the secluded peninsula of Upper Saranac Lake. It is one of the few lodges continuing the tradition of the great camps of the Adirondacks.

Everything about The Point points toward its opulent history. The huge timbers used to construct the living room roof were brought in from Canada. Gigantic boulders form the large fireplaces in the Great Hall. The property includes two acres of lake frontage and seven acres of wooded land. The guest quarters are eleven rooms in several different buildings, lodges, cabins, and boathouses scattered around the property for privacy. Each room has a lake view, custom-made bed, and bath with chrome and brass fixtures. The accommodations are furnished in the Adirondack style with lots of exposed wood and a rustic simplicity. Make sure to get a room with a fireplace.

"We try to make our guests feel that they have come to a house party in the woods," says owner Christie Garrett. This feeling is reinforced by service with attention to details. Your day at The Point begins with a soft knock on the door and morning coffee, served in a thermos so you can take your time enjoying it. Later, a slightly bolder knock announces the arrival of breakfast. You can have the meal in bed, at your breakfast table overlooking the lake, or before the fire on a chilly morning.

Outdoor activities abound. You can go canoeing, rowing, sailing, or water-skiing on the lake. Swimming is also popular, in the crystal clear fresh water. Take a hike on The Point's nature trails, or, if you're looking for bigger mountains to climb, venture out into the vast Adirondacks. For those who have more civilized sporting tastes, golf and tennis is available at the nearby country club. The Point is a great place to stay for a winter ski vacation, with many downhill mountains and excellent cross-country trails within easy reach.

Lunch is served on the terrace outdoors or packed into baskets for picnics at the lakeside or on one of the many islands dotting the lake. The dining room, supervised by Chef Albert Roux, of Gavroche in London, is only open to paying guests. Jacket and tie is required for dinner, where the guests sit together at a great table, just like a formal dinner party. Candlelight and fresh flowers decorate the table, and classical music plays in the background. Wednesday and Saturday dinners are black tie optional affairs. After dinner, enjoy an apéritif in the Great Hall or take one of The Point's regular sunset cocktail cruises on the lake.

Children under eighteen are not allowed, which lets the adults enjoy a little peace and privacy.

Rates: $825–$1,300 (all meals, open bar, and recreation included)

THE POINT
HCR #1 Box 65
Saranac Lake, NY 12983

Phone	(518) 891-5674
Toll free	(800) 255-3530
Fax	(518) 891-1152

North Carolina

THE GREYSTONE INN
Lake Toxaway

> The mind has a thousand eyes,
>   And the heart but one;
> Yet the light of a whole life dies
>   When love is done.
>
> — "The Night Has a Thousand Eyes"
>   by Francis William Bourdillon

People who have visited The Greystone Inn tell others not to publicize it; they'd rather keep it their own little secret. But it's too good a place not to share.

Picturesquely situated on Lake Toxaway in the Blue Ridge Mountains of western North Carolina, this luxury resort was originally a private estate. Now it offers a wide range of recreational activities and four-star cuisine in the quiet splendor of rural beauty.

The lobby is decorated with antique furnishings and period reproductions. The walls are paneled in oak, and there's a large stone fireplace overlooking the terrace and Lake Toxaway, North Carolina's largest private lake. There are thirty-four rooms at The Greystone, but no suites. Twenty of the rooms are in the main mansion, the rest are spacious lakefront rooms in Hillmont, a separate structure adjoining the mansion. Make sure to ask for a room with a view of the lake and a working fireplace. All the rooms, each named after a noteworthy individual who played a key role in the region's history, have cable television and whirlpools.

The restaurant is superb, serving six-course American regional dinners of the highest quality. Look out onto the mountains and golf course while you dine at tables sparkling with candlelight and fresh flowers. Live piano or guitar music accompanies your meal. There's also regular live entertainment and a piano bar in the cocktail lounge. Afternoon tea is served on the Sun Porch, filled with comfortable wicker furniture. Cocktails may be enjoyed in the richly appointed Library or outside on the North Terrace overlooking the lake. Every day at sunset you can join the owner for a party boat cruise on the twenty-eight-foot Mountain Lily II.

The Inn is a fully equipped recreational resort with an outdoor pool, six tennis courts, a championship golf course, sailing and waterskiing on the lake, jogging and hiking trails on the 5,000 private acres, excellent fishing, and a massage spa. Tennis instruction is available on site.

Rates: Rooms $245–$495

THE GREYSTONE INN
Greystone Lane
Lake Toxaway, NC 28747

Phone	(704) 966-4700
Toll free	(800) 824-5766
Fax	(704) 862-5689

Ohio

THE CINCINNATIAN
Cincinnati

> It is not while beauty and youth are thine own,
>   And thy cheeks unprofaned by a tear,
> That the fervor and faith of a soul may be known,
>   To which time will but make thee more dear!
>
> — "Believe Me, If All Those Endearing Young
>   Charms" by Thomas Moore

In a city not usually associated with romance, The Cincinnatian is making a reputation for itself. The hotel originally opened in 1882, but a $23 million facelift has left it anything but old fashioned. Now it's a European style hotel with modern details mixing comfortably with the original architecture.

The atrium lobby is stunning evidence that the renovation was a success. The hotel's original walnut and marble grand staircase has been preserved and rises into the contemporary furnishings of the atrium. You might like the looks of the atrium enough to request a room with a flower-decked balcony that faces out onto it.

There are two restaurants at The Cincinnatian. The Palace features new American cuisine and is one of Cincinnati's finest restaurants. The restaurant is setting standards for impeccable classic service, with dishes presented under silver domes, and an impressive wine selection. The Cricket Lounge, at the base of the atrium lobby, serves lighter fare and has a piano bar. Afternoon tea is served at the Cricket Lounge, and the pastries are superb. In fact, the ritual is getting so popular that local businesspeople now talk of "power teas" at The Cincinnatian.

Celebrities are beginning to make The Cincinnatian the hotel of choice in the Queen City. The Rolling Stones have stayed here, as have New Kids on the Block. It's located right in the center of downtown Cincinnati, just off Fountain Square, the city's traditional business, shopping, and entertainment center.

The hotel offers packages for romantic couples. There is a special celebration on Valentine's Day. During the rest of the year, the Incurable Romantic Weekend package includes deluxe accommodations, continental breakfast, champagne, and welcome basket, turndown service including a long-stemmed rose, and discounts on food and beverages.

Rates: Rooms $195–$245; Suites $400–$1,500
(based upon season)

THE CINCINNATIAN
601 Vine Street
Cincinnati, OH 45202

Phone   (513) 381-3000
Toll free   (800) 942-9000
Fax   (513) 651-0256

Oregon

COLUMBIA GORGE HOTEL
Hood River

> Whether in the bringing of the flowers or of the food
> She offers plenty, and is part of plenty,
> And whether I see her stooping, or leaning with the
>   flowers,
> What she does is ages old, and she is not simply,
> No, but lovely in that way.
>
> — "Part of Plenty" by Bernard Spencer

Situated on the green banks of the Columbia River Gorge in Hood River Oregon, this is a great place to experience the natural splendor of the Pacific Northwest. Just an hour east of Portland, the Gorge is a setting of exquisite dramatic beauty. The hotel first opened in 1921 and quickly developed an international reputation for elegant hospitality amidst rugged beauty. Presidents Roosevelt and Coolidge were visitors, as were Myrna Loy and Jane Powell. It's rumored that Rudolph Valentino and Clara Bow used the Columbia Gorge as a romantic hideaway.

The hotel sits near the base of Mt. Hood with the 206 foot Wah-Gwin-Gwin Falls in the hotel's backyard. Recently renovated, the hotel's forty-six rooms and public areas have been designed to allow the gorgeous surrounding scenery pour inside. One of the most amazing meals you'll ever see is "The World Famous Farm Breakfast" where you can gorge yourself. This is what they serve (and it's not a choice, you get it all): seasonal fruits, apple fritters with sugar and spice, old fashioned oatmeal with brown sugar and sweet cream, three farm fresh eggs, bacon, smoked pork chop, apple and maple flavored sausage, hash browns, powder biscuits and honey, a stack of buttermilk pancakes with hot maple syrup, and coffee. Of course you can also enjoy a breakfast drink from their outstanding selection of champagne and other cocktails.

If you're every hungry again, there's a fantastic dinner menu, including items like fresh Columbia River salmon in lemon-butter Chardonnay sauce and grilled medallions of venison. And save room for the apple tart, Columbia Gorge. A rich butter caramel sauce blended with Hood River apples, thinly sliced and baked under a covering of puff pastry, served hot with French vanilla ice cream.

Travel writers have called the hotel, "one of the most romantic places on Earth," and it's easy to see why. The spectacular views and lush gardens, fantastic food, and rural seclusion make this a romantic's dream spot. The Columbia Gorge Hotel is a great place to have a wedding, featuring five different reception rooms and a varied banquet and hors d'oeuvres menu. And the hotel has its own in-house florist to take care of flower arrangements.

Rates: Rooms $150–$270; Suites $295–$365

COLUMBIA GORGE HOTEL
4000 Westcliff Drive
Hood River, OR 97031

Phone   (503) 386-5566
Toll free   (800) 345-1921
Fax   (503) 387-5414

THE HEATHMAN HOTEL
Portland

> My love is such that rivers cannot quench,
> Nor ought but love from thee, give recompense.
> Thy love is such I can no way repay,
> The heavens reward thee manifold, I pray.
> Then while we live, in love let's so persevere
> That when we live no more, we may live ever.
>
> — "To My Dear and Loving Husband"
>   by Anne Bradstreet

If you're looking for spectacular service in elegant surroundings, The Heathman is the place to stay in Portland. An atmospheric blend of old and new, of laid back comfort and refined luxury, of East meets West, The Heathman offers the best of both worlds.

The lobby is a sumptuous space, decorated with an Italian marble floor, Burmese teak walls and seventeenth-century Japanese antiques. Of the 150 rooms in the hotel, forty are suites. But only about ten rooms (and six suites) have views. Be sure and ask for a room on the 9th or 10th floor, with a west hills view. Fresh plants and original artwork by local artists add a pleasant touch to each room. The mirrored and marbled bathrooms are extra large for intimacy and comfort. All rooms are equipped with televisions and VCRs, and a huge video library containing over four hundred movies for use free of charge. But the most impressive library is the collection of books the Heathman maintains, many of them signed first editions by authors who have stayed at the hotel.

The Heathman Restaurant and Bar serves northwest regional cuisine, classically prepared and attractively presented. Candlelight adorns the tables and recorded classical music plays in the background. You can also reserve one of the seven quiet private dining rooms on the mezzanine. Afternoon tea is served in the historic Lobby Lounge every day and live piano music accompanies cocktail hour afterwards. The Lounge regularly features live jazz, which you can also hear from the overlooking Mezzanine Bar.

The staff at The Heathman says, "There are a couple of places to spend a perfect weekend. The other one is Paris." And they try hard to back up this claim with a splendid Perfect Weekend package, which includes dinner for two in the romantic restaurant (or breakfast in bed), valet parking, transportation to the best theaters and concert halls in town, a complimentary gift, and accommodations. They also offer Honeymoon and Anniversary packages that include champagne served in keepsake glasses and room-service meals.

The Heathman is located right in the heart of

beautiful Portland. It's next door to the Performing Arts Center and just around the corner from the Oregon Art Institute. Pioneer Place is only a couple blocks away. Celebrities and performers are discovering The Heathman. Recent guests include Mikhail Barishnikov, Neil Diamond, Leontyn Price, and Jay Leno.

Rates: Rooms $140–$180; Suites $185–$225

THE HEATHMAN HOTEL
S.W. Broadway at Salmon
Portland, OR 97205

Phone	(503) 241-4100
Toll free	(800) 551-0011
Fax	(503) 227-5607

Pennsylvania

FOUR SEASONS HOTEL
Philadelphia

> Love hath power over princes
>   And greatest emperor;
> In any provinces,
>   Such is Love's power,
> There is no resisting,
>   But him to obey;
> In spite of all contesting,
>   Love will find out the way.
>
>   — "Love Will Find Out the Way," Unknown

Often overwhelmed by its sister cities along the Atlantic coast, Philadelphia is an unappreciated gem. The cultural attractions are world class, with an excellent art museum and one of the best orchestras in the world. Center City has a dynamic nightlife, and the residential neighborhoods of Society Hill and Rittenhouse Square offer a elegant respite from urban stress. You can visit the many historic sights, including the Liberty Bell, or enjoy the latest novelties in cuisine or entertainment. As W.C. Fields once said, "On the whole, I'd rather be in Philadelphia."

And the best place to stay in Philadelphia is the Four Seasons Hotel. There are 371 rooms in this massive hotel, but only eight suites. All the rooms are decorated in the Federal style, reflecting the same decor in the common rooms of the hotel. The Presidential Suite has a large marble bathroom with a whirlpool.

Candles and fresh flowers decorate the tables in the dining room. Live music plays throughout the day, ranging from classical to jazz. After dinner go for a romantic walk to the Swann Fountain in nearby Logan Square. Viennese dessert buffet is served on Friday and Saturday nights from 9 p.m. until 1 a.m. in the morning.

In addition to delectable pastries and sinful desserts, you can dance to the trio playing in the Swann Lounge.

The Four Seasons offers a romantic Honeymoon package. Upon checking in, honeymooners register their names on the Florentine marbelized pages of the hotel's wedding registry. A special table is set overlooking the Swann Fountain and Logan Circle, fresh strawberries covered in chocolate and champagne are served. The king-sized bed is turned down and dressed with a soft white sheet and duvet. A single long-stemmed rose lies upon the lace boudoir pillow. After that the lovebirds are left alone until room service breakfast the next morning. And the hotel's town car will take them on to the airport or train station for the next stop in their new life together.

Rates: Rooms $270–$345; Suites $625–$1,750

FOUR SEASONS HOTEL
One Logan Square
Philadelphia, PA 19103

Phone   (215) 963-1500
Toll free   (800) 332-3442
Fax   (215) 963-9506

THE INN AT TURKEY HILL
Bloomsburg

> Our share of night to bear,
> Our share of morning,
> Our blank in bliss to fill,
> Our blank in scorning.
>
> Here a star, and there a star,
> Some lose their way.
> Here a mist, and there a mist,
> Afterwords—day!
>
>   — "The Lovers" by Emily Dickinson

Emily Dickinson could have been describing an overnight visit to The Inn at Turkey Hill, a family-owned and operated hideaway in rural Bloomsburg. Located in central Pennsylvania, the Inn is perfect for romantic escapes from either Pittsburgh or Philadelphia, or even as a destination from further away.

The Inn has eighteen separate accommodations, each one individually decorated. The cottages and suites have fireplaces and jacuzzis. The main building, originally built in 1839, and the other structures overlook a landscaped courtyard with seasonal flowers, duck pond, gazebo, and pastoral walking paths. The patio is a great place to sit back and unwind.

There are three separate dining rooms at the Inn, and the food is superb. Dinner entrées can include rolled duck with wild cherry sauce or veal Oscar served by candlelight. Lunch is served at the Tavern, or you can enjoy it out on the gazebo or patio. Complimentary continental breakfast is served in the sunny Greenhouse every morning. The Inn offers special Honeymoon and Anniversary packages, including champagne and flowers, a cheeseboard, and continental breakfast in one of their fabulous suites.

Located on the Susquehanna River, Bloomsburg is halfway between the Appalachians and the Poconos. There's a lot to do in the surrounding area. Learn how to fly fish or go golfing or skiing at local facilities. Tour the surrounding countryside, which has almost as many covered bridges as Madison County. Go for a walk through Bloomsburg's historic district or catch a show at the town's theater ensemble.

Rates: Rooms $92; Suites $145–$185

THE INN AT TURKEY HILL
991 Central Road
Bloomsburg, PA 17815

Phone   (717) 387-1500
Fax   (717) 784-3718

THE PRIORY
Pittsburgh

> Unlace yourself, for that harmonious chime,
> Tells me from you, that now it is bedtime.
>
> Your gown going off, such beauteous state reveals,
> As when from flowery meads th'hill's shadow steals.
>
> Now off with those shoes, and then safely tread
> In this love's hallow'd temple, this soft bed.
>
> Licence my roving hands, and let them go,
> Before, behind, between, above, below.
>
> To enter in these bonds, is to be free;
> Then where my hand is set, my seal shall be.
>
> — "To His Mistress Going to Bed" by John Donne

A pleasant alternative to bustling Pittsburgh, The Priory offers the kind of peace and quiet that's not often found in downtown hotels. Once a home for Benedictine monks, The Priory has now become a home-away-from-home for business travelers and weekend visitors to the Steel City. Here you can enjoy the comforts of a nineteenth-century inn with the conveniences of a modern hotel.

The red brick building is designed with Romanseque-arched windows and parapeted gables. And its maze of rooms and corridors is positively Gothic. But the guest accommodations are thoroughly up-to-date, and each room is individually decorated with Victorian furnishings.

While The Priory does not have a restaurant, they do serve a hearty continental breakfast, replete with home-baked bread, muffins, coffee cakes, cereals, fresh fruits and juices, and of course, great coffee. Sit and sip complimentary wine by the fountain. In the winter, sip port or sherry in front of the fireplace in the sitting room.

The Priory is conveniently located across the Allegheny River from the Golden Triangle of downtown Pittsburgh. It's only a half mile from downtown and offers a spectacular view of the city skyline—which you can't see if you're right in the middle of it. During the week, complimentary limousine service is provided to downtown. The neighborhood of East Allegheny, or "Deutschtown" as it is also known, is a historic district now in a stage of redevelopment. Right near the hotel is a variety of cultural offerings, including the shops and boutiques of Allegheny Center, the picturesque homes of The Mexican War Streets, the Buhl Science Center, the Pittsburgh Public Theater, and Three Rivers Stadium.

What if you don't feel like going anywhere? Then perhaps you can follow the instructions of that great devout, John Donne.

Rates: Rooms $65–$130; Suites $105–$150
     (based upon season)

THE PRIORY
614 Pressley Street
Pittsburgh, PA 15212

Phone   (412) 231-3338
Fax   (412) 231-4838

▬▬▬

South Carolina

CHARLESTON PLACE
Charleston

> To cheat the eyes
>   of stern
> leering prudes
> adds honey to
>   love's cup.

> — "Our Kisses" by Paulos

Charleston is a spectacular city, rich with history and timeless beauty. Horse-drawn carriages make their way down cobblestone streets that lead to some of America's most beautifully preserved antebellum homes, antique shops, museums, and piazzas. Every spring the town comes alive with celebrations, most notably the Spoleto Festival, a world-class performing arts marathon that attracts performers and fans from all over the globe to this exquisite gem of a city. Whether you're here for Spoleto or any other time of year, the place to stay is Charleston Place.

Modern day Rhetts and Scarletts, guests of Charleston Place, are swept into tradition in the reception area of the hotel, embraced by a grand, curving double staircase lit by an enormous crystal chandelier. Upstairs the 440 rooms and forty suites provide guests with elegant period-style furnishings, ceiling fans, and opulent bathrooms with Botticino marble and glass fixtures. Premier accommodations crown the two top floors where The Club offers a higher level of luxury service. Here you will enjoy a private elevator, concierge service, special check-in and check-out privileges, and complimentary food and cocktails.

Relaxation and recreation begin at the Fitness Center where a retractable glass roof allows year-round sunning

and swimming in the heated indoor pool. A fully
equipped exercise room, steam room, and sauna are also
available. Or you can soak in the huge jacuzzi while overlooking the view of downtown Charleston.

Southern Living calls afternoons in the Lobby Lounge
"the best known of tea times in the city." Evenings in the
Lounge are nearly as famous, when hors d'oeuvres,
cocktails, and desserts are served to the accompaniment
of live piano music. Louis' Charleston Grill offers unique
Low Country cuisine. Here you can dine in a relaxed
atmosphere and ambiance entertained by a wonderful
jazz trio and vocalist. The Palmetto Cafe is another popular dining room which features breakfast and brunch buffets during the weekends.

Charleston Place spares no effort in entertaining its
guests with fine southern hospitality and has earned a
reputation as one of the finest hotels in the Carolinas.

Rates: Rooms $275–$295; Suites $325–$1,500

CHARLESTON PLACE
130 Market Street
Charleston, SC 29401

Phone	(803) 722-4900
Toll free	(800) 611-5545
Fax	(803) 722-0728

JOHN RUTLEDGE HOUSE INN
Charleston

> Then be not coy, but use your time,
>   And while ye may, go marry:
> For having lost but once your prime,
>   You may forever tarry.
>
> — "To the Virgins, to Make Much of Time"
>   by Robert Herrick

Another great place to stay in Charleston is the John
Rutledge House Inn. Home of John Rutledge, one of the
signers of the U.S. Constitution, the house has been
called "America's most historic inn" and is protected as a

national historic landmark. Originally built in 1763, the house has been faithfully restored to retain all the exquisite architectural details of its original construction, while still providing all the safety and comfort of a modern facility. The Inn is located right in the heart of Charleston's historic district.

A great deal of Charleston history happened in the ballroom and library of this grand old house. John Rutledge was truly one of this country's founding fathers. In addition to signing the Constitution, Rutledge served as chief justice of both the U.S. and the South Carolina Supreme Courts, governor of South Carolina, commander in chief of the South Carolina militia during the Revolutionary War, and delegate to the First and Second Continental Congresses. George Washington had breakfast here at John Rutledge's house.

The Inn has nineteen guest quarters spread among a complex of three buildings. You can choose between the classic elegance of suites in the original residence or the charm and seclusion of rooms in the two carriage houses. Antiques and historic reproductions decorate all the rooms, some of which have fireplaces.

In the afternoon and evening, partake of southern hospitality as wine and sherry are served in the ballroom. At the end of the evening, you'll find chocolates and a nightcap awaiting you in your room. In the morning, both continental and full breakfasts are available. And the Inn is near Charleston Place, the Market, and a host of restaurants and shops.

Rates: Rooms $150–$230; Suites $215–$310

JOHN RUTLEDGE HOUSE INN
116 Broad Street
Charleston, SC 29401

Phone   (803) 723-7999
Toll free   (800) 476-9741
Fax   (803) 720-2615

VENDUE INN
Charleston

> Then a mile of warm sea-scented beach;
> Three fields to cross till a farm appears;
> A tap at the pane, the quick sharp scratch
> And blue spurt of a lighted match,
> And a voice less loud, thro' its joys and fears,
> Than the two hearts beating each to each!
>
> — "Meeting at Night" by Robert Browning

Another fantastic place to stay in Charleston is the Vendue Inn. There are forty-five rooms in the Vendue, twenty-three of which are suites. All the rooms are decorated in eighteenth-century style furnishings featuring poster and canopy beds, oriental carpets, and old Charleston fabrics and wall coverings. Guests receive coffee liqueur at bedtime and continental breakfast in the morning, in addition to fruit baskets and a fully stocked bar, all complimentary. Fresh flowers are kept in every room. The suites are much larger than the other rooms (which can be a bit small) and they have spacious marble bathrooms, elegant dining rooms, and lovely bedrooms. The suites also have jacuzzis and fireplaces, and most of them have a view of Charleston Harbor.

But the best view of the harbor is found on the roof terrace, which also rises above the other roofs of the city. Wine and cheese are served in the afternoon, accompanied by chamber music. And the old English library is a cozy place to curl up with a good book and a glass of sherry. The restaurant, The Library, has candle-light and fresh flowers at dinner, with recorded chamber music. Serving "cuisine of the new world", The Library offers such entrées as shrimp in coconut milk Leeward Islands style and beef tenderloin medallions flamed in Jack Daniels.

The Vendue is run by the husband and wife team, Morton and Evelyn Needle, and they do their best to personalize the service. "I never wanted this to be a hotel," Evelyn says, "I wanted people to feel like guests in my own home." And many of their guests do feel right at home. The Vendue is a regular stop for many political and cultural leaders visiting Charleston.

Rates: Rooms $115–$155; Suites $145–$225
     (based upon season)

VENDUE INN
19 Vendue Range
Charleston, SC 29401

Phone   (803) 577-7970
Toll free   (800) 845-7900
Fax   (803) 577-2913

Tennessee

THE PEABODY
Memphis

> Wine comes in at the mouth
> And love comes in at the eye;
> That's all we know for truth
> Before we grow old and die.
> I lift the glass to my mouth,
> I look at you, and I sigh.
>
> — "A Drinking Song" by W. B. Yeats

The Peabody is one of the grand hotels of the South. Visit Memphis and you can't help notice it, right in the center of town, a grand old dowager that has withstood the test of time and is now even more beautiful than ever. It's the kind of place you feel instantly at home. Even among the luxurious surroundings, southern hospitality shines through.

The most famous residents of The Peabody are, of course, the ducks. Back in the 1930s, the general manager of the hotel came back from a hunting trip with a couple of live decoys and thought they might like to swim in the fountain pool. He didn't know he was starting a tradition, which continues to this day. Now the ducks march down to the lobby every morning at eleven, and later return to their pen at the Royal Duck Palace up on the hotel's roof. To make their march more stately, the staff rolls out a red carpet and plays John Philip Sousa's "King Cotton March."

But there's more than just waterfowl to The Peabody. Conveniently located in the middle of downtown Memphis, the hotel is the absolute best place to stay in this fascinating city. Right across the street is the Rendevous, the best barbecue restaurant in a town of great barbecue. The Peabody is also convenient to the Cotton Exchange, Mud Island, Beale Street, and other Memphis attractions.

Chez Phillipe at The Peabody is one of the finest restaurants in the region. *The New York Times* said the restaurant alone was worth a special trip to Memphis. Harp music plays softly in the background as you enjoy classic French cuisine in an elegant setting. Cafe Dux offers award-winning American cuisine in a setting of contemporary decor. Cafe Expresso, a cross between a New York deli and Viennese dessert shop, is open late for snacks. You can enjoy cocktails at a variety of different spots, each with its own unique charm: the famous Lobby Bar, up on the Plantation Roof with a stunning view of the city and the mighty Mississippi, the Club Bar, Mallards, or the art deco Skyway.

The Peabody offers a special Touch of Romance package. Upon arrival, you and that special someone receive cold champagne and fresh flowers, followed by cocktails in the Mallards or Lobby Bar. The next morning you'll be served champagne brunch either in the privacy of your own room or on the Skyway, with a spectacular view of the city.

"The Mississippi Delta begins in the lobby of The Peabody and ends on Catfish Row in Vicksburg. The Peabody is the Paris Ritz, the Cairo Shepheard's, the London Savoy." Historian David Cohn wrote this in 1935 and it's still true today.

Rates: Rooms $130–$310; Suites $595–$1,345

THE PEABODY
149 Union Avenue
Memphis, TN 38103

Phone   (901) 529-4000
Toll free   (800) PEABODY (732-2639)

Texas

LA COLOMBE D'OR
Houston

> I told my love, I told my love,
> I told her all my heart;
> Trembling, cold, in ghastly fears,
> Oh! She doth depart.
>
> — "Never Seek to Tell Thy Love" by William Blake

Nothing compares to La Colombe D'Or. This unique and spectacular prairie-school style residence was first built in 1923. Then Steve Zimmerman turned it into a European-style boutique hotel. Zimmerman calls his pleasure palace "the smallest luxury hotel in the world." And in this case, small is good, especially when you want peace, quiet, privacy, and personalized service.

The hotel has only six guest rooms, and a staff of thirty-six, so you can imagine the level of attention you'll enjoy here. Some of the suites are residences all to themselves. The Degas Suite, for example, has an intimate dining room decorated with a French crystal chandelier, and Queen Anne chairs.

Chef Olivier Ciesielski is an artist, supervising a restaurant that produces authentic French cuisine served with impeccable style. Fresh seafood is brought in daily by local fishermen from the Gulf, and many of the herbs used in the menu dishes are grown in La Colombe D'Or's own herb garden. Start with a cocktail in the wood-paneled library or the Bacchus Bar. The restaurant does not turn over tables, so when you reserve a table, it's yours for the whole evening. Instead of being rushed through the several courses of a fine French meal, you'll be allowed to relax and savor both the food and the atmosphere of the elegant dining room. Rich desserts are a specialty here.

La Colombe D'Or is located in the artsy Montrose district of Houston. It's close to most of the city's attractions, particularly the Museum of Fine Arts, the Contemporary Arts Museum, Rice University, and the unavoidable Astrodome. But once you walk into this beautifully appointed little jewel of a hotel, you might never want to leave your room.

Rates: Rooms $195–$275; Suites $575

LA COLOMBE D'OR
3410 Montrose Blvd.
Houston, TX 77004

Phone   (713) 524-7999
Fax   (713) 524-8923

THE FOUR SEASONS HOTEL
Austin

> Darling, each morning a blooded rose
> Lures the sunlight in, and shows
> Her soft, moist and secret part.
> See now, before you go to bed,
> Her skirts replaced, her deeper red—
> A colour much like yours, dear heart.
>
> — "Corinna in Vendome" by Pierre de Ronsard

Located in the heart of downtown Austin, just a short ride away from the state capitol, the University of Texas, and the L.B.J. Library, The Four Seasons is a great place to stay, whether you're in Austin for a romantic weekend, or you're there on a business trip and want your surroundings to be as romantic as possible.

The Four Seasons is consistently ranked as the best hotel in Austin. The atmosphere is distinctly Texan, with the service and amenities that you've come to expect from Four Seasons' Hotels. But this hotel is more laid back than others in the chain. The lobby is warm and comfortable, with a large fireplace and lots of luxurious furniture to relax in. Have a drink in the Lobby Lounge, and watch the people go by. There are 291 rooms in the hotel, all of them offering amenities like concierge service, twenty-four-hour room service, terry-cloth bathrobes, and complimentary newspapers. But the best accommodations are the executive suites.

The hotel is nestled on the banks of Town Lake, with its park land surroundings, and hiking and biking trails. Enjoy a swim in the heated outdoor pool overlooking the lake. The fully equipped health club includes saunas, whirlpool, and other facilities.

The Four Seasons offers some of Austin's finest restaurants. The Cafe features a lakeside terrace, where imaginative American and southwestern cuisine is served. The terrace is a great perch for bat-watching, a favorite Austin pastime. And it's also a popular place among locals for Sunday brunch.

At night, check out the exciting night scene on Austin's famous 6th Street. Live music from country to jazz to "grunge rock" is played (often without cover charges) in the street's countless bars and nightclubs.

Rates: Rooms $195–$240; Suites $245–$425

THE FOUR SEASONS HOTEL
98 San Jacinto Boulevard
Austin, TX 78701

Phone	(512) 478-4500
Toll free	(800) 332-3442
Fax	(512) 477-0704

▬▬▬▬

THE MANSION ON TURTLE CREEK
Dallas

> Come quickly—as soon as
> these blossoms open,
> they fall.
> This world exists
> as a sheen of dew on flowers.
>
> — "Come Quickly" by Izumi Shikibu

Caroline Rose Hunt has created several of the best hotels in America, among them the Hotel Bel Air in Los Angeles.

And The Mansion on Turtle Creek is one of her crowning achievements. Consistently ranked as one of the top hotels in the world by a wide range of travel authorities, The Mansion is an exquisite place. It is particularly appealing to romantics because of the fine attention to detail, exceptional restaurants, and superlative service.

There are 128 rooms in this Mansion, and fourteen of them are suites which happen to be simply stunning. Individually decorated with original art, the suites have a living room, two bedrooms, wet bars, separate powder rooms, and a full kitchen. Suites on the ninth floor have roof gardens with a view of the Dallas skyline. Bathrooms feature marble shower stalls and vanities, custom brass fixtures, and large dressing areas. Room service offers a full menu, so you never have to leave your room.

Set on a low rise above meandering lawns, The Mansion is situated near the neighborhood of Highland Park. It has all the feel of a private residence, which isn't suprising, because that's what it initially was. And the pace at The Mansion is like you are the guest at a country home. There's plenty to do nearby, but no one will force you to do anything. Instead you are encouraged to take it easy, to simply enjoy the surroundings and amenities. At The Mansion you are pampered with prompt, personal attention. But when you wish to be left alone, you are. This is a place just to be, to sleep until noon if you feel like it, to wake up only for breakfast in bed followed by a lounge by the pool.

Then there's dinner to look forward to. The restaurant at The Mansion is one of the finest in the country. Chef Dean Fearing is recognized as the founding father of haute southwestern cuisine, combining the regional flavors of Native American, Spanish, Mexican, Southern, and American cowboy cookery to produce a unique and unparalleled menu. Specialties include lobster taco, tortilla soup, salad with smoked salmon, and roasted quail.

According to a reader's poll in *D Magazine,* a local Dallas magazine, The Mansion was the best restaurant in Dallas. It was also judged the most romantic: "From the quick takeover of your car by beaming attendants to the ritual welcome at the *maître d' station,* right on through exquisite service of fine fare and wines in a setting of no-stone-unturned splendor, dinner a *deux* here is an evening to remember." The same survey said The Mansion served the best desserts. Fearing is so confident that no one can make crème brûlée as well as he can that he even made his secret recipe public.

After dinner, relax in the lounge and get a hand-written weather report for the next day. But you don't need to decide right then whether you want to sleep in.

Rates: Rooms $290–$391; Suites $495–$1,350

THE MANSION ON TURTLE CREEK
2821 Turtle Creek Boulevard
Dallas, TX 75219

Phone	(214) 559-2100
Toll free	(800) 527-5432
Fax	(214) 528-4187

THE TREMONT HOUSE
Galveston

> Mine eye to like her face doth lead.
> Mine ear to learn her tongue doth teach.
> My heart to love her wit doth move.
>
> — "Her Face" by Arthur Gorges

Every few years a hurricane comes along and tries to wipe Galveston off the map, but it will take more than just a few natural disasters to take away the beauty and charm of this Gulf Coast city. Galveston is a historic island that maintains its Victorian charm well into the twentieth century. And The Tremont House is a long-standing tradition in this town of great history.

Back in the days when Galveston was a bustling harbor, The Tremont House was the city's leading hotel. It continues to be so today. The historic landmark building is situated right in the enchanting Strand district of Galveston, convenient to all the shops, galleries, and restaurants of this exciting quarter.

The hotel has been recently renovated. Now there are 111 rooms in this grand old lady. The guest rooms are furnished in Victorian decor, with high ceilings, ceiling fans, brass beds, heated towel warmers, and complimentary Crabtree & Evelyn toiletries. If you want a view, The Tremont offers several. We recommend the city or harbor view, depending on whether you prefer lights or water.

There are two restaurants, the intimate Merchant Prince and the more formal Wentletrap. Candlelights and fresh flowers adorn the tables at the Wentletrap, where a dress code is enforced. Sunday brunch at the Wentletrap can include such delicacies as Trout Almondine and Redfish Grenobloise. Dinner features entrées like fresh Gulf shrimp en brochette or Chateaubriand. The Tremont also has two piano bars and a lounge. Afternoon tea is served daily, as is champagne in the evening.

For activities, the hotel offers an outdoor pool, tennis courts, golf, horseback riding, fishing, and a private beach. All these are located off the premises of this historically preserved area, but the staff provides transportation to allow their guests to enjoy them. Lady Bird Johnson and Helen Hayes were both frequent guests at The Tremont, along with many prominent Texans.

Rates: Rooms $99–$185; Suites $200–$375

THE TREMONT HOUSE
2300 Ship's Mechanic Row
Galveston, TX 77550

Phone	(409) 763-0300
Toll free	(800) 874-2300
Fax	(409) 763-1539

Utah

STEIN ERIKSEN LODGE
Park City

> Love's not Time's fool, though rosy lips and cheeks
> Within his bending sickle's compass come,
> Love alters not with his brief hours and weeks,
> But bears it out even to the edge of doom:
>> If this be error and upon me proved,
>> I never writ, nor no man ever loved."
>
> — "Let Me Not" by William Shakespeare

Utah ski resorts don't get the attention that their glitzy cousins in Colorado receive, and for many that's part of their charm. Sure, there's not as lively a night scene in predominantly Mormon Utah, but that doesn't mean you can't make your own excitement.

The Stein Eriksen Lodge is one of the premier ski lodges in Utah. Forty-five minutes from Salt Lake City, the lodge is nestled in the alpine splendor of the Deer Valley Resort at Park City. The Lodge is on the mountainside, and most of the rooms have a view of the mountain (make sure to ask for one). About half the rooms have fireplaces. The suites also have spacious decks. The rooms are decorated in Scandanavian color and theme. Bathrooms are equipped with oversized whirlpools. And the lobby has a huge stone fireplace, where afternoon tea is served accompanied by piano music. Candlelight and fresh flowers are a regular feature in the Glitretind Gourmet Room, where the menu is superb. There's a state wine and liquor store in the Lodge with an excellent wine selection. Remember, there are strict liquor laws in Utah, but the staff will keep you from running afoul of them.

Other amenities include a heated, year-round swimming pool, a health spa with exercise room, sauna, hot tub, and massage rooms. There's also a sports shop, and ski rental and repair shop for your equipment needs. You can buy a lift ticket right at the desk and ski out to Deer Valley's Sterling lift. And the outdoor walkways are heated so you don't get chilled coming in or going out.

Celebrities eager to enjoy mountain solitude have taken advantage of the Stein Eriksen's impeccable hospitality. Folks like Dustin Hoffman, Ann Margaret, Sidney Poitier, Bruce Springsteen, and Gerald Ford have stayed there, and although it's made its reputation as a ski resort, don't dismiss Stein Eriksen when planning a summer vacation. The summer days in the mountains are warm and dry, with virtually no humidity. Nights are cool enough for a sweater, with a sky full of stars. Summer events in the area include rodeos, concerts, and sports competitions.

Rates: Rooms $149–$650; Suites $225–$2,500
      (based upon season)

STEIN ERIKSEN LODGE
P.O. Box 3177
Park City, Utah 84060

Phone	(801) 649-3700
Toll free	(800) 453-1302
Fax	(801) 649-5825

Vermont

TWIN FARMS
Barnard

> Love at the lips was touch
> As sweet as I could bear;
> And once that seemed too much;
> I lived on air.
>
> — "To Earthward" by Robert Frost

You can almost live on air in Vermont. Whether you visit in the glorious fall, spectacular summer, colorful spring, or snowy winter, the Green Mountain state is the perfect antidote to civilization, without giving up any of its pleasures.

Consistently ranked as one of the top resorts of the region, Twin Farms is quickly establishing a reputation for exquisite surroundings, personalized service, private lodgings, and great cuisine. Once the honeymoon home of novelist Sinclair Lewis and journalist Dorothy Thompson, Twin Farms is 255 acres of rolling hills, meadows, orchards, gardens, woods, and ponds in central Vermont.

The original 1795 main house has been transformed into a central complex of guest rooms, dining areas, and living rooms. Surrounding the main house are finely detailed guest cottages, a handsome pub with fitness center, and a separate building featuring a Japanese furo bath.

The food at Twin Farms is superb. Head Chef Neil Wigglesworth, formerly chef at The Point, provides seasonally changing cuisine. Continental breakfast is delivered in wicker baskets to your suite or cottage, or you may enjoy a full breakfast in the main house. Lunch can be taken in the dining room, on the terrace, or as a barbecue, clambake, or picnic outdoors. Following cocktails at 7 p.m., dinner is served at 8 p.m. Dinners may be taken individually or *en famille* in a variety of locations around the property. You can then retire to the Barn Room for an array of local and European cheeses served with selected ports and cordials. During the summer, cognac is served by a roaring bonfire over by Copper Pond.

If you want to keep busy, there are plenty of sporting activities. In the winter, downhill skiing is available on the Farm's own groomed slopes. Major resorts such as Killington and Pico are also nearby. The lake is tended so you can ice skate. Or you can take a sleigh ride, wrapped in quilts and warmed by flasks of mulled wine. In the summer, there's canoeing, swimming, fishing, tennis, and croquet. A Robert Trent Jones golf course is minutes away at the Woodstock Country Club. Hiking and walking trails lead to remote forest settings.

Of the fourteen guest accommodations, four are private suites in the Main House, two share a large cottage nearby, and the others are free-standing cottages scattered across the property for maximum privacy. Each guest quarter has at least one fireplace, and all are individually decorated, most with antique furnishings. The king-sized feather beds earned *Hideaway Report's* "Best, Most Inviting Hotel Beds, Anywhere."

Rates: Suites and Cottages $700–$1,800
       (based upon season)

TWIN FARMS
P.O. Box 115
Barnard, VT 05031

Phone   (802) 234-9999
Toll free   (800) TWINFARMS (894-6327)
Fax   (802) 234-9990

Virginia

MORRISON HOUSE
Alexandria

> With thee conversing I forget all the time,
> All seasons and their change, all please alike.

— *Paradise Lost* by John Milton

It's nice to have a place where you can leave time behind, even if you're minutes from the nation's capital, where the clock is always ticking. The Morrison House is located in the lovely, historic neighborhood of Old Town Alexandria, just across the Potomac River from Washington, D.C. Once home to Robert E. Lee and other Virginia gentry, Old Town has been revitalized without losing its quaint, historic character. Filled with well-maintained townhouses along the residential streets, and a stunning variety of shops and restaurants in the commercial district, Old Town has a perfect blend of charm, convenience, and creature comforts.

The place to stay in Old Town is the Morrison House. Located on South Alfred Street, the Morrison House has forty-five rooms, three of which are suites. The guest quarters are individually decorated in Federal Period authentic reproductions, including poster beds and custom-made armoires. Each room is provided with fresh Virginia peanuts (which many claim are the best in the country), top-shelf cosmetics, and current magazines.

There are two restaurants in the Morrison House. Elysium serves spectacular, contemporary, and upscale American cuisine. And The Grille is a piano bar, offering more down-to-earth fare. Tables have candlelight and fresh flowers and there is piano music to accompany your dinner. And if you don't feel like leaving the privacy of your room, twenty-four-hour room service is available. Afternoon tea is served daily.

From the moment the butler greets you at the door, you'll be treated like visiting royalty in an atmosphere of gentility and quiet elegance. Concierge service will meet all your special needs, including transportation to nearby National Airport or tickets to Washington events. The Morrison House has an indoor pool and massage spa, and exercise room with weights and aerobics.

The Morrison House offers several special packages, including Honeymoon and Romantic Getaway packages, which offer complimentary champagne, breakfast in bed, and other luxurious amenities.

Regular visitors to Washington find the Morrison House a pleasant refuge from the nation's capital, while being almost as convenient as a downtown hotel. Famous visitors include Joan Baez, Morgan Fairchild, Ben Davidson, and a recent Miss USA.

Rates: Rooms $150–$240; Suites $295

MORRISON HOUSE
116 South Alfred Street
Alexandria, VA 22314

Phone	(703) 838-8000
Toll free	(800) 367-0800
Fax	(703) 684-6283

THE INN AT LITTLE WASHINGTON
Washington

> Yet come to me in dreams, that I may live
>> My very life again though cold in death:
> Come back to me in dreams, that I may give
>> Pulse for pulse, breath for breath:
>>> Speak low, lean low,
> As long ago, my love, how long ago
> — "Echo" by Christina Rossetti

The Inn at Little Washington is one of the most beautiful country inns in Virginia, and one of the best restaurants as well. The Inn is famous for its innovative cuisine and pastoral setting. It's a favorite gathering spot for

Washington-types looking to get away from it all and the local squirearchy looking to get in on the action. Craig Claiborne celebrated his sixty-fifth birthday here. Former Senator Eugene McCarthy and syndicated columnist James J. Kilpatrick are regulars (they live nearby).

Each of the Inn's ten rooms is furnished like a grand Victorian country house. Cookies, fruit, and a bucket of ice make your room instantly comforting. The marble bathrooms have heated towel racks for your comfort. Afternoon tea is brought to your room. In the morning, *The Washington Post* is left outside your door. After reading the paper, a house breakfast for two is served downstairs. There are two two-level suites available. The first level has a beautiful parlor decorated with exquisite antiques and hand-painted wallpaper. The parlor features a wet bar and stereo for your relaxation and pleasure, as well as a balcony. The first level also has a dressing area with a jacuzzi and a shower. The second level has a king-size bed and two separate balconies—one facing the garden and the other with a sitting area to enjoy your afternoon tea. Because the Inn is such a popular romantic retreat, you might have to make reservations well in advance. But it will be well worth the wait.

Breakfast at the restaurant can include pan-broiled local trout along with freshly squeezed juices, and hot rolls. Chef Patrick O'Connell is one of the hottest culinary talents on the eastern seaboard. He always uses the freshest ingredients, including home-grown produce in season. And the menu can be incredibly innovative, with items like shad roe served with grapefruit. The wine list includes bottles from France, California, and Virginia vineyards. The best table at the restaurant is number 66, a private space at the end of the enclosed porch, surrounded by two gardens.

The town of Washington can claim to be the only place named after George Washington before he became president. (He surveyed the area in 1749.) This Washington is only sixty-seven miles away from the other Washington. The surrounding countryside is dotted with gorgeous horse farms and parklands. Skyline

Drive and the Blue Ridge mountains are just minutes away.

Rates: Rooms $250–$540; Suites $410–$675

THE INN AT LITTLE WASHINGTON
P.O. Box 300
Middle and Main Streets
Washington, VA 22747

Phone   (540) 675-3800
Fax   (540) 675-3100

WILLIAMSBURG INN
Williamsburg

> But our love it was stronger by far than the love
> Of those who were older than we—
> Of many far wiser than we—
> And neither the angels in Heaven above,
> Nor the demons down under the sea,
> Can ever dissever my soul from the soul
> Of the beautiful Annabel Lee.
>
> — "Annabel Lee" by Edgar Allan Poe

The historic town of Williamsburg is a breathtaking trip back to Colonial America. The attention to detail is so exquisite that if it weren't for the tourists taking pictures, you might think you were in the 1700s, when Williamsburg was the capital of Virginia and a hotbed of the revolution. The town features real stores with the goods for sale back then and shows off artisans practicing crafts (like wigmaking) that have long gone out of fashion.

If you have a passion for history, then Williamsburg is the place for you. And the Williamsburg Inn is the place to stay in this historic burg.

Of course the Inn reflects the historical accuracy of Williamsburg itself. The lobby is decorated in Regency style, with fireplaces at each end. From the lobby you can look out onto the terrace and golf course. The musical instruments played in the dining room can be anything from harp to piano to string trio. Candles and fresh flowers are always in the dining room, where the entrées can include noisettes of beef tenderloin with fresh oysters or venison in a pepper cream sauce. Two cocktail lounges give you an option for drinks before and after dinner.

But there are also plenty of modern comforts and conveniences, like an indoor and an outdoor pool, tennis courts, and a massage salon. The Golden Horseshoe Golf Course is right outside. And lawn bowling is also available. A few steps from the lobby of the Inn, and you're in Colonial Williamsburg.

The lodgings at the Inn include a total of 235 guest quarters. Many of those rooms are in the Inn itself. But the real experience is to stay in one of the Colonial houses. The houses are situated in the heart of the restored area. Decorated with period furnishings, they still have all the modern conveniences. Many celebrities and world leaders have stayed at the Colonial houses, including the heads of several countries during the 1983 Summit of Industrialized Nations. But you don't have to run a country in order to enjoy the quaint charm of these historically accurate houses.

Rates: Rooms $255–$365; Suites $435–$750
       Colonial Houses $185–$840 (based upon season)

WILLIAMSBURG INN
P.O. Box B
Williamsburg, VA 23187

Phone	(804) 229-1000
Toll free	(800) HISTORY (447-8679)
Fax	(804) 220-7096

Washington

THE ALEXIS HOTEL
Seattle

> How long such suspension may linger? Ah, Sweet,
> The moment eternal—just that and no more—
> When ecstasy's utmost we clutch at the core,
> While cheeks burn, arms open, eyes shut, and lips
> meet!
>
> — "Now!" by Robert Browning

The Alexis Hotel is a small, classy hotel, the kind you can get real comfortable in real quickly, and yet never forget that you're someplace special. It's a hotel in the style of a residential European hostelry—simple, elegant, with impeccable service.

There are 109 rooms in The Alexis, of which forty-two are suites with whirlpool baths and wet bars. Eight of the suites have working fireplaces. None of the rooms have much of a view, except of the courtyard. But you can get plenty of vistas as you see the rest of Seattle.

The lobby is decorated with a marble front desk and antique furnishings, including a baby grand piano and brass elevators. Upon arrival you receive a welcome sherry. At night, turndown service includes homemade chocolates. Continental breakfast is complimentary, and you get a choice of three morning newspapers. There is a no-tipping policy for bellmen, valets, and housekeepers.

In a serene, spacious and stylish art gallery setting, The Painted Table serves elegantly simple New American cuisine. Emphasis is on locally-grown herbs and vegetables, fresh seafood, and regional specialties. Executive Chef Tim Kelley is classically trained with strong Asian and French influences. After a memorable dinner you can enjoy the live pianist performing nightly in the lobby. The Bookstore, located at the hotel's First Avenue

155

entrance, serves light lunches, appetizers, and desserts, in addition to its full beverage service. The Bookstore features a collection of international magazines and cookbooks to browse through.

The Alexis Hotel has won numerous awards through the years: the Mobil Four Star Award, 1984–1996; AAA Four Diamond Award, 1984–1996; and American Express Platinum Card Fine Hotels and Resorts, 1991–1996.

Rates: Rooms $175–$210; Suites $220–$360

THE ALEXIS HOTEL
1007 First Avenue at Madison
Seattle, WA 98104

Phone   (206) 624-4844
Toll free   (800) 426-7033
Fax   (206) 621-9009

▬▬▬

THE SALISH LODGE
Snoqualmie Falls

> If thou must love me, let it be for nought
> Except for love's sake only. Do not say
> 'I love her for her smile—her look—her way
> Of speaking gently.'
>
> — "If Thou Must Love Me, Let it Be for Nought"
> by Elizabeth Barrett Browning

What is it about waterfalls that makes the atmosphere so romantic? Some scientists claim that the water mists put an electrical charge in the air, but that takes the mystery out of the allure of cascading water. Some things are better left unexplained. If you like waterfalls but don't want to brave the crowds at Niagara, try the Salish Lodge at Snoqualmie Falls, the "Niagara of the West."

Located about a half hour east of Seattle, The Salish is situated at the crest of the magnificent Snoqualmie Falls, offering a unique combination of comfort and style in an elegant country inn designed to complement the spectacular natural setting. The falls plunge 268 feet—that's more than one hundred feet farther than Niagara.

The Lodge has ninety-one guest rooms with custom-designed furniture, luxurious bedspreads, and down comforters. The walls of each room are paneled in native straight fir, and the floors are made of northwestern slate. All rooms have stone-faced wood-burning fireplaces, two-person whirlpool spa tubs with French doors opening out onto the room and the spectacular view beyond. Most rooms have balconies or patios overlooking the river. There are four suites with parlors and extra bedrooms.

You can relax in the Curtis Library, named after Asahel Curtis, a turn-of-the-century photographer whose original photos are featured in the library. Or go shopping at the Salish Country Store, featuring designer clothing and accessories and original northwestern art. The Salish fitness center is located on the roof, offering an outdoor spa and sun deck, sauna, and state-of-the-art exercise equipment. Cuisine at The Lodge features regional game, fish and fowl, and an extensive wine list.

There are two lounges. The Falls Terrace opens onto a large outdoor terrace overlooking the falls. The sweeping panorama of the Attic Lounge, located on the roof level, features nightly live entertainment and dancing, as well as some of the Northwest's best light jazz and mood music. Sporting activities include golf, fishing, biking, hiking, rock climbing, horseback riding, and cross-country or downhill skiing. Or you can take an unforgettable helicopter picnic and enjoy great Northwest cuisine atop the scenic Mt. Si. The nearby town of Snoqualmie was the inspiration (and provided some of the locations) for David Lynch's avant-garde *Twin Peaks* television series.

Salish offers a honeymoon special. A romantic riverside room, champagne served in keepsake glasses, and breakfast in bed, all which help to set a romantic mood.

Rates: Rooms $180–$210; Suites $500–$575
    (based upon season)

THE SALISH LODGE
6501 Railroad Avenue, S.E.
Snoqualmie, WA 98065

Phone	(206) 831-6502
Toll free	(800) 826-6124
Fax	(206) 888-2533

THE SORRENTO HOTEL
Seattle

> I love thee with the passion put to use
> In my old griefs, and with my childhood's faith.
> I love thee with a love I seemed to lose
> With my lost saints,—I love thee with the breath,
> Smiles, tears, of all my life!—and, if God choose,
> I shall but love thee better after death.
>
> — "How Do I Love Thee? Let Me Count the Ways"
>   by Elizabeth Barrett Browning

Misty, moist Seattle offers some of the most dramatic scenery and one of the most stimulating urban environments in the country. On a clear day you can see Mt. Rainier, and even when it's cloudy (it rains three hundred days out of the year), it's still a beautiful city.

On your visit, you can explore the city itself, go to the top of the Space Needle, or go shopping at Pike Place Market. Sip espresso in one of the hundreds of coffee bars. Take in a concert at the Seattle Symphony or a play at one of Seattle's thriving theater companies. Or you can use Seattle as a base to explore the surrounding area— Puget Sound and San Juan Islands or the rugged coastline of the Pacific Northwest.

The Sorrento is conveniently located on the first of Seattle's seven hills (like another great city, Rome). In fact, The Sorrento was inspired by Italian Renaissance villas, and the architecture is meant to convey both warmth and style. The hotel has an intimate appeal. There are only seventy-six rooms, of which forty-two are suites. All of the rooms are tastefully and uniquely decorated, giving each a personality all of its own. When the hotel was renovated in 1990, the newly refurbished suites won several awards from travel experts. The Penthouse Suite offers a sweeping view of Seattle and Mt. Rainier.

Fine dining is served at the Hunt Club Restaurant, and piano entertainment is provided almost every night. The Hunt Club is famous for new American cuisine served in a mahogany-paneled dining room that has the feel of an English club. Entrées might include rack of lamb with loganberry wine sauce and eggplant turnovers filled with lamb sausage.

The Sorrento offers a romantic Honeymoon/Anniversary package. You get a deluxe suite with champagne upon arrival. The next morning enjoy continental breakfast in your suite or in the cozy Hunt Club. Valet parking is included. The deluxe Romance package includes all of the above plus an individually crafted floral arrangement by The Sorrento's in-house florist, and a horse-drawn carriage ride through town. The Romance package rates range from $250 to $450.

Rates: Rooms $160–$180; Suites $200–$1,200

THE SORRENTO HOTEL
900 Madison Street
Seattle, WA 98104

Phone	(206) 622-6400
Toll free	(800) 426-1265
Fax	(206) 625-1059

West Virginia

THE GREENBRIER
White Sulphur Springs

> What do I wish to do?
> I wish to love:
> that verb at whose source all verbs
> take fire and learn to move.
> Yes, could I rightly love,
> all action, all event,
> would from my nature spring
> true as creation meant.
> Love takes no pains with words
> but is most eloquent.
>
> — "Wishes" by Judith Wright

The Greenbrier is one of the most famous resorts in the country, and deservedly so. A favorite getaway for the Washington power elite, this spectacular retreat is a sprawling establishment set on 6,500 acres in the gorgeous Allegheny Mountains of West Virginia.

In operation for more than two hundred years, The Greenbrier has a long-standing tradition of outstanding hospitality. Many of the staff can claim two or even three generations of service at the resort. And some of the chefs are home-grown as well, graduates of the famous Greenbrier Culinary Apprenticeship Program.

The Greenbrier offers a wide range of sporting activities. You can jog, hike, or ride horseback over the miles of woodland mountain trails. There are three eighteen-hole golf courses and twenty tennis courts. Fishing, as well as trap and skeet shooting, are also available. A full service spa and mineral bath service help revitalize your aching muscles and leave the pressures of life behind you.

But The Greenbrier is not a spa, and the food and beverage service is both generous and exquisite. Tea is served in the afternoon, accompanied by live chamber music. Cocktails in the White Club are a must, followed by dinner in the elegant Main Dining Room, where the tables are decorated with fresh flowers, candlelight flickers, and a string ensemble plays romantic music. Later, return to the White Club for more music and dancing. In the morning, don't worry about being awakened early. Before 9 a.m. the staff actually whispers so as not to disturb their guests.

The Greenbrier offers a wide variety of rooms and suites—in the hotel, as well as in guest houses—with up to four bedrooms. All the hotel rooms have beautiful views of the gardens and grounds. But only the guest houses have fireplaces. The guest houses also offer privacy and comfort, wide porches with awnings and wicker furniture to enjoy an afternoon cocktail overlooking some of the most beautiful areas of the resort. The houses have full room service so you don't have to ever venture from beyond the front porch, if you don't want to. But if you do, the houses are conveniently located to all the resort's many sport and leisure activities.

The Greenbrier offers special Honeymoon and Anniversary packages. They include accommodations, breakfast and dinner in the elegant Dining Room, happy hour hors d'oeuvres in the Old White Club, evening movies, dancing, swimming, a hotel tour, complimentary champagne, flowers, and a color photograph to cherish the memories.

Rates: Rooms $416–$520; Suites $660–$4,970
      Guest Houses $600–$2,000 (based upon season)

THE GREENBRIER
White Sulphur Springs, WV 24986

Phone	(304) 536-1100
Toll free	(800) 624-6070
Fax	(304) 536-7854

Wisconsin

THE AMERICAN CLUB
Kohler

> Eyes were made for beauty's grace,
> Viewing, rueing love's long pain,
> Procur'd by beauty's rude disdain.
>
> — "To His Love" by Anonymous

Consistently ranked as one of the top resorts, not just in the Midwest but throughout the country, The American Club offers luxury and elegance in a friendly atmosphere. Looking at the gorgeous landscaping and gardens, and the stately tudor architecture, you'd never think that the Club was originally built for the immigrant workers employed by Kohler in 1918. Carefully refurbished in 1981, the Club was reopened as a luxury hotel.

The resort area features nine restaurants, four of which are in the Club. The Immigrant Restaurant is the Club's premier dining room. Serving dinner only, the Immigrant features international cuisine and fine wines, and has been named one of the top restaurants in North America. The adjacent Winery is a comfortable place to enjoy cocktails and fine wines by the glass. Live entertainment is offered on the weekends. The Club's original dining room has been transformed into the elegant Wisconsin Room Restaurant, where breakfast, lunch, and dinner are served amid oak paneling, antique chandeliers, leaded glass panels above French Doors, and original tapestries. The Greenhouse is a charming antique solarium brought over from England and reconstructed here. Now it's a delightful cafe in the fountain courtyard, a great place for afternoon and evening refreshments, including a tantalizing variety of desserts, pastries, coffees, and specialty drinks. Health conscious diners can partake at the Jumping Bean, which overlooks the indoor pool. In the summer a floating dining terrace—the Marine Bean—is set on scenic Wood Lake. The Horse and Plow is a casual pub with turn-of-the-century ambiance.

Blackwolf Run, the resort's two eighteen-hole golf courses, offers challenges for duffers of all skill levels. *Golf Digest* ranked the River Course among the top one hundred courses in the country, and the fourth best public course. The Blackwolf Run Cluhouse looks out onto panoramic views of the river valley, providing a comfortable atmosphere for year-round dining or relaxing after a game of golf. River Wildlife, the resort's five hundred-acre wilderness preserve, offers a rustic retreat plus trails and a meandering river for outdoor activities. Sports Core is a private health and racquet club offering a full-service spa, tennis, swimming, and other recreational activities. Nearby are the shops at Woodlake Kohler, offering a variety of specialties in a scenic lakeside setting.

The American Club offers a special Romantic Interlude package. You get two night accommodations, breakfast in your choice of restaurants or room service, an intimate dinner at any of the restaurants, complimentary champagne in keepsake glasses, American Club chocolates, and a single, exquisite rose in a vase. The rates for this package range from $695 to $1,125, depending on when you visit and what type of lodging you choose.

Rates: Rooms $170–$250; Suites $270–460
    (based upon season)

THE AMERICAN CLUB
Highland Drive
Kohler, Wisconsin 53044

Phone	(414) 457-8000
Toll free	(800) 344-2838
Fax	(414) 457-0299

THE PFISTER HOTEL
Milwaukee

> Small is the worth
> Of beauty from the light retired:
> Bid her come forth,
> Suffer herself to be desired,
> And not blush so to be admired.

— "Go, Lovely Rose" by Edmund Waller

The Pfister is a gorgeous gem of a hotel. First opened in 1893, this historic building has retained its romantic charm while modernizing enough to maintain its status as Milwaukee's most luxurious lodging. This mix of convenience and history is emulated in the hotel's buildings themselves, a landmark original structure complemented by a modern twenty-three story tower.

The Pfister boasts the largest collection of late eighteenth-century artwork owned by any hotel in the world. And the collection is generously distributed throughout the hotel. All the guest rooms are decorated with English country furniture in Queen Anne style. Bathrooms are finished in Italian marble. Suites come with a marble and glass wet bar, and five of them offer private whirlpools.

The top floor of the hotel's modern tower features a health club with a swimming pool. Massages are available to invigorate and revitalize those tired muscles. If that's not enough, membership privileges at the Downtown Club are offered to Pfister guests.

Also on the top of The Pfister tower is the La Playa cocktail lounge, where you can enjoy a spectacular view of downtown Milwaukee while sipping a cocktail, munching on generous hors d'oeuvres, or dancing to live music. The English Room is the hotel's formal restaurant, featuring elegant cuisine and a fabulous wine list. The glass-enclosed verandah of Cafe at the Pfister is a great place to eat breakfast, lunch, or a late-night snack. Cafe Rouge is a cocktail lounge off the main lobby, serving weekday lunch and Sunday brunch accompanied by live music. The Lobby Lounge, which is located on the historic lobby level, is open for cocktails and offers live piano nightly.

The Pfister is located in the East Town area of downtown Milwaukee, close to the many shops and stores. It's also convenient to the financial district and only a short walk to Lake Michigan and most of the cultural events this surprising city has to offer.

Rates: Rooms $225–$250; Suites $265–$700

THE PFISTER HOTEL
424 East Wisconsin Avenue
Milwaukee, WI 53202

Phone	(414) 273-8222
Toll free	(800) 558-8222
Fax	(414) 273-8082

Wyoming

JENNY LAKE LODGE AT GRAND TETON NATIONAL PARK
Moran

> Love, ah Love, when all your slipknot's drawn,
> We can but say, 'Farewell, good sense.'
>
> — "The Lion in Love" by Marianne Moore

Grand Teton National Park is one of the most spectacular natural settings in the country. The Grand Tetons, Jackson Lake, and the National Elk Refuge all create unparalleled wild scenery. Nearby is the south entrance to Yellowstone Park and millions of acres of wilderness forest land.

In your explorations of this gorgeous area, you need a home base with some of the essentials of civilization, like four-star cuisine. And Jenny Lake Lodge is the place to enjoy all the pleasures of refined comfort in this rough yet beautiful country. A resort committed to providing its guests with elegant service in a rugged location, the lodge is owned by CSX, which also operates Colter Bay Village.

Lodging at the Jenny Lake is in a series of cabins on the property. Each cabin is simply furnished, but with all the modern conveniences. Electric blankets and hand-made quilts add to your comfort on the cool mountain evenings. Privacy was the prime concern in building the cabins, and they all have porches to enjoy the dramatic view.

The food at Jenny Lake is excellent regional cuisine prepared with a classical touch. The menu might include such Rocky Mountain favorites as broiled buffalo steak with herb butter or sautéed local trout. The chef makes sure to prepare several menu items with fewer calories, low sodium, and low cholesterol for visitors who are watching their diets. For those who are not, there are plenty of goodies available, from escargot to deep fried ice cream. Sunday night buffets are a specialty.

Of course there is a lot to do around Jackson Hole. You can go rafting down the rapids of the Snake River. Horseback riding is included in the room rates, and the lodge offers breakfast rides, afternoon wagon rides, and evening rides concluded with a marshmallow roast. Tennis and golf are at the nearby Jackson Hole Club. The town of Jackson itself is filled with lots of interesting shops and attractions, including the world famous Cowboy Bar.

Rates: Cabins $335; Cabin Suites $470–$480
      (Open from June 1–September 28)

JENNY LAKE LODGE AT GRAND TETON NATIONAL PARK
Highway 89
Grand Teton National Park
P.O. Box 240
Moran, WY 83013

Phone   (307) 733-4647
Fax   (307) 543-2869

If you have a favorite romantic resort that you would like us to consider for our second edition of *Bed & Champagne,* please send us your suggestions. Also, if you have something to add to the resorts that are included in this edition, or you believe we missed the target on any resort, please let us know.

I'd also like to hear your answer to the age-old question—what is romance?

Boru Publishing
12004-B Commonwealth Way
Austin, TX 78759